THE ROAD TO MOSCOW

Manchester
EveningNews

at heart ♡ publications
www.atheart.co.uk

First published in 2008 by
At Heart Ltd
32 Stamford Street, Altrincham, Cheshire, WA14 1EY

in conjunction with
Manchester Evening News
1 Scott Place, Hardman Street, Manchester, M3 3RN

© 2008 Manchester Evening News
Some images supplied by PA Photos/AP

ISBN: 978-1-84547-213-9

Printed and bound by Bell & Bain, Glasgow.

CONTENTS

SPORTING LISBON v MANCHESTER UNITED

PRE-MATCH

Cristiano Ronaldo is preparing himself for an emotional welcome back to Sporting Lisbon as United kick off their 2007-08 European campaign in Portugal.

But Sir Alex Ferguson is worried that his star winger isn't receiving such warm treatment from referees.

The United manager has been expressing concern that the 22-year-old 2007 double Footballer of the Year has been targeted by referees and has become the victim of his success.

Ronaldo was sent off at Portsmouth in August and on his return from his three-match ban at Everton the weekend before the trip to Lisbon, he was booked for diving. Fergie's mood and concern was not eased when he learned in the pre-match press conference that German official Herbert Fandel was to take charge of the Group F opener in the Jose Alvalade Stadium.

Fandel had sent off Roy Keane and Paul Scholes in previous Champions League seasons. When he was informed that Fandel was UEFA's choice for the match Fergie asked: "Have you got a supply of Mogadon?"

Ferguson hoped Fandel would be calm in Portugal but Ronaldo's Goodison yellow card was a major fear for Fergie.

Ronaldo, however, preferred to remain tight-lipped on the subject. Sat alongside his manager at the press conference he said, "I only speak about this with my manager and my team. I don't speak about referees now.

"What the boss says is true. But my focus is on the game to keep my concentration and do my best for United and not about the referee. I don't want to speak about that."

The Reds winger has had a torrid time returning to Portugal in the past against Porto and twice against Sporting's arch-Lisbon enemies Benfica.

A gesture to Benfica fans in December 2005 led to a one-match ban imposed by UEFA. But he was expecting a warm welcome back from the club and fans he had left as an 18-year-old in August 2003 to play for United in a £12.5m deal.

"It is always good to come back," the Madeiran added.

"I wouldn't say it is my home but it is my second home. I had seven years here and I have a lot of friends here and colleagues.

"I think the people at Sporting like me. It is different to going to play Benfica. At Benfica everyone booed me but that is in the past. I think my reception here will be good.

"I like the club and respect them but my first colour now is red and I aim to win. I think we are the better team. I will do my best and am not sure how I will feel out there.

"If I score I don't know how I will react!"

United had kept tabs on the teenage Ronaldo even before the pre-season friendly four years ago, which saw the winger destroy United at the opening of the Jose Alvalade Stadium.

Fergie immediately fast tracked the transfer.

Ronaldo said prior to his return: "That was a spectacular match. I've watched it several times. It was the first game in the new stadium in front of a full house against United, a team I had always dreamed of playing for.

> *"I don't need memories of that night as inspiration. I believe in my strength and motivation as it is. I can't wait."*

Ferguson ended in bullish mood: "We hope to re-establish ourselves in Europe. We have the ability and last year we showed that."

Owen Hargreaves was a Champions League winner with Bayern Munich in 2001 and predicts an open tournament with United among the best bets for success in Moscow.

"The amount of individual talent we have at United is bigger than we had at Bayern when we won the Champions League," he said.

"What we did at Bayern was defend well and counter-attack well. The Champions League is similar to all major tournaments where teams tend to be cautious and don't want to risk losing matches because there aren't many games.

"At United, we will play offensive, attractive football. That's what we want to do. We will play attractive football and I am sure we will be extremely successful.

"There are some fabulous teams in the Champions League. It is harder than ever before.

"There are more clubs capable of winning it now. When we won it at Bayern in 2001, there were a few teams who could be successful.

"But now every English team in the competition has the potential to win it.

"Then you have Inter, AC Milan, Barcelona and Real Madrid. Real have improved extremely well. The balance of the competition is very good.

"However, United are one of the favourites. In my opinion possibly the major favourites would be Manchester United, Barcelona, Real Madrid and the holders AC Milan.

"But then you have Chelsea and Liverpool who have shown to be very difficult to beat in Europe as well. It is very open."

PREMIERSHIP TOP FOUR PRE SPORTING LISBON SEPT 19							
	P	W	D	L	F	A	PTS
Arsenal	5	4	1	0	10	4	13
Manchester City	6	4	0	2	5	2	12
Liverpool	5	3	2	0	11	2	11
UNITED	6	3	2	1	4	2	11

United's final-week preparations for the defence of the 2007 League title was an ironic build up to the start of the Premiership campaign.

The last Old Trafford warm up had a Champions League feel about it with Inter Milan visiting. The Reds lost 3-2 with the back five being turned over by the Italians.

"Our defending in the first half was very poor, and we will not win games no matter who they are against, if we defend like that," said an unimpressed Sir Alex Ferguson.

Five days later in the Community Shield at Wembley they beat Chelsea on penalties!

The Reds finally saw through the two-year loan deal of Carlos Tevez after his summer transfer saga on the eve of the League season.

United, though, were slow out of the blocks and suffered a number of critical blows.

They drew at home to Reading 0-0 on the opening day of the season and Wayne Rooney suffered a hairline fracture of his left foot.

The Reds drew 1-1 at Portsmouth where Cristiano Ronaldo was sent off and had to serve a three-match ban.

Then they lost the derby at Eastlands against Manchester City.

After just three games crisis talk was in the air.

But the title-holders rallied to go into the first Euro trip of the campaign against Sporting Lisbon with three successive 1-0 victories against Spurs and Sunderland at Old Trafford and Everton at Goodison.

However, they suffered another blow when they lost Mikael Silvestre to a cruciate knee ligament injury against Everton.

Ten months before his Moscow European Cup trophy clinching penalty saves, Edwin Van der Sar gave a spooky sneak preview of his heroic finale in May.

In the Community Shield on August 5, against their ultimate Champions League Final opponents Chelsea, the Dutchman saved spot kicks from Claudio Pizarro, Frank Lampard and Shaun Wright-Phillips to win the curtain-raiser silverware at Wembley.

"I have never saved three penalties in a row before," said the Dutchman.

"It has been done before, I remember Helmuth Duckadam saving all four for Steaua Bucharest in the 1986 European Cup Final against Barcelona.

"That was a little bit of a bigger thing to win than the Community Shield but we are happy with this one anyway."

Your big prize would come, Edwin!

CHELSEA CAPTAIN JOHN TERRY ON UNITED'S POOR LEAGUE START

"I would have expected United to have started a bit better but a lot of clubs have bought really well over the summer. Five points is a hell of a gap to have this early on. It's going to be difficult for United."

AUGUST 3 – UNITED FINALLY SIGN CARLOS TEVEZ AFTER TRANSFER SAGA

After months of uncertainty, Carlos Tevez has at last signed for Manchester United.

Sir Alex Ferguson commented: "Over the years most of our signings have been successful, so I think our judgement is good.

"There has also been good evidence on which to judge Carlos. His profile with Argentina is good, and we started watching him when he was 18 years of age.

"Then he played for the Olympic team when he was 20 and we watched him progress from there to national level. But without question it was his performances last year in the Premier League that were the foundation on which this transfer was based.

"There are no doubts in my mind that his performances and contribution to West Ham last season saved them from relegation. I watched most of the run-in, and winning seven of your last nine games is championship form. The platform was there for him to use and he used it fantastically well, showing what a truly world-class player he is.

"When he played against us in the last league match of last season, I didn't know what his contract situation was – I don't think anyone knew the implications.

"But we have been watching Carlos for a long time and when a deal became possible last summer it was way too complex.

"With Javier Mascherano going to Liverpool towards the end of last season it clarified the situation for us and in a way helped us to decide to go for Carlos."

AUGUST 15 – RONALDO SENT OFF AT PORTSMOUTH

Christiano Ronaldo picked up a red card against Portsmouth following an apparent headbutt.

Ferguson said: "I have tried to look at the replay and there was nothing conclusive there. In fact you cannot really see anything. But my take is he was provoked and he has fallen for it.

"Cristiano was responsible for falling into the trap of intimidation which has happened to him a few times again. He has only himself to blame and it left us with only ten men and he'll be missing for three games now. It is a big blow."

Ferguson, though, had grave concerns for his star player.

"There is every chance Cristiano could get a serious injury," he said.

"I don't know if there is a directive but I have noticed over the last few months, referees seem to be more tolerant of physical contact.

"A lot of late challenges have gone unpunished and at Portsmouth that happened time and time again.

"I don't know whether referees have been instructed to manage these situations but to me, it is black and white.

"That does not mean players should get away with doing stupid things on the pitch, but there is a concern players like Ronaldo are going to be the victims.

"Cristiano fell for a 100-year-old trick but it is very difficult to completely punish him or to be angry with him because some of the things that happen to him are not right."

AUGUST 28 – 1999 EUROPEAN CUP HERO OLE GUNNAR SOLKSJAER RETIRES

Solskjaer was finally forced to hang up his boots after a losing battle against persistent knee problems.

The Norwegian striker said: "I would like to thank the manager, the coaching and medical staff, and most of all the supporters, who have supported me through my career.

"They have been fantastic and were a real inspiration to me when I was out injured.

"I have had the best education ever at United and I want to let others have the benefit of that. Now it's time to teach others.

"When you have major operations and you think your career is being taken away from you, you begin to think of ways to stay in football and coaching is what I want to do. I have had it in my mind for a while now.

"Obviously, I wanted to play on but, when the knee blew up again last week and I realised I'd reached the end of the line and couldn't play at the level I wanted to and what the manager needed for Manchester United, I had an easy decision really and it was time to look forward."

Sir Alex Ferguson said: "Ending your playing career is a sad day for anyone, in the case of Ole, he has 11 fantastic years he can look back on.

"Ole has achieved everything a player could ever wish to achieve.

"He has been a great servant to the club and has always

We hope lessons will have been learned about what happened because someone could have been killed. It is amazing no one was killed.

"Our fans took appalling abuse and the scenes were sickening.

"It is a reminder to us that we need our fans to be vigilant and behave well when we meet again. They should not be intimidated. Just go to the game, enjoy it and cheer the team. That's what I expect them to do."

Old Trafford chief executive David Gill added: "What we need to do is do our homework and work very closely with Roma.

"I'm sure the lessons have been learned by Roma and the authorities from last year. We believe our fans acted very properly and were found to be broadly blameless.

"I think we need to all work together to ensure the game is remembered for what happens on the field as opposed to off it.

"We will discuss it with Roma and UEFA to make sure it is remembered for what happens on the field and make sure everyone travels in safety."

SEPTEMBER 3 – REPORTS OF A BILLION POUND POTENTIAL TAKEOVER OF UNITED FROM CHINA AND DUBAI

The Glazer family insist they won't be packing up and cashing in on United, despite reports of potential billion-pound takeovers from China and Dubai.

A Chinese consortium is said to be keen to invest in the world's biggest club and develop the commercial market in Asia.

Reports also say a rival Arab group, with connections to the Emirates royal family, is working in the background and considering a move on Old Trafford.

But United's American owners are adamant they don't want to do business.

A spokesman for the Florida-based family said: "I can state unequivocally that United are not for sale.

"The Glazer family is 100 per cent committed to long-term investment and ownership in the club. Their commitment has been demonstrated by the expenditure during the transfer window. The position has not changed and nor will it.

"They have only owned the club for two years and this is still very much the beginning. It's business as usual."

remained a model professional in his responsibility as a player, in his demeanour and his manners have always been exemplary."

Solskjaer remains at United as an ambassador and has been appointed reserve team manager.

AUGUST 31 – UNITED DRAW ROMA IN GROUP F

After the horrific terrace scenes in the Olimpico Stadium in April at the quarter-final tie, Sir Alex Ferguson hopes lessons have been learned after United were pitched in against the Italians again in the Champions League group draw

Ferguson said: "What disturbed us at the time when we saw video footage was that all the police were in the Manchester United section.

"There were no police in the Roma fans' section. So therefore they were able to hurl all sorts of objects at our supporters.

"There should be equal control of both sets of fans.

Edwin Van der Sar was winning the Champions League with Ajax before Cristiano Ronaldo had even left Madeira to join Sporting's productive academy as an 11-year-old.

Ronaldo's homecoming turned into a match-winning evening for the ex-Sporting Lisbon youngster. But it was the veteran Dutchman who really became United's hero in this match as the Reds stretched their obsession for 1-0 victories to four in a row after identical Premiership wins against Spurs, Sunderland and Everton leading up to this Champions League Group F opener.

There was a lot of emotion attached to this particular European campaign for United, with both Old Trafford knights Sir Bobby Charlton and Sir Alex Ferguson stressing the poignancy of success in Moscow in May as a fitting tribute to the victims of Munich 50 years ago.

The Reds needed to significantly improve if they were to carry that burden all the way to Russia and deliver the touching homage.

Although a difficult start to United's European adventure, the team emerged victorious from the confrontation.

Fergie's team had everything going for it as the Reds boss plumped for players with individual goals driving them on.

He could no longer keep Wayne Rooney on the leash after his swift recovery from the broken foot sustained in the opening League match against Reading.

Then you had Ronaldo returning to the club that nurtured him for seven years, hoping to show his ex-support just why he took England by storm last season.

Nani, another product of the burgeoning Sporting Academy who had left for Old Trafford during the summer, was also back on home soil. But none of these talented players could find the spark in the first half, suggesting United's abysmal away form in the Champions League since 2004, which saw them win just two matches out of 14, wasn't going to statistically improve as the competition progressed.

Rooney must have been somewhat frustrated that having left behind the treatment room and training ground for the real thing, he found himself pretty much a lone figure in the Reds' attack.

Nani didn't do anything to convince the hierarchy at his former club that they had made the wrong decision in their brokering of the £17m deal for the 20-year-old.

You also wonder if Ronaldo is fuelled by jeers that assault his ears at all the away grounds back home in the Premiership.

Here in the Jose Alvalade Stadium, the home crowd may have cheered every time he was dispossessed but

it was certainly a respite from the vicious catcalls he gets in England.

His moment of glory looked a distant hope after an uninspiring first period, when there was little of the show-stopping form Ronaldo showed here in August 2003 that convinced the Reds to get him onto the Old Trafford payroll pronto.

Serbian Nemanja Vidic had been detailed to keep close tabs on Sporting's danger man Liedson.

A first-minute clash of heads and the United tough nut hit the Brazilian striker with a sledgehammer challenge which didn't register on Vidic's pain barometer but laid out Liedson.

The South American is clearly made of stern stuff because he refused to be intimidated or retreat from the firing line and proved why he is such an effective threat.

It was his curling 28th-minute right footer that was the pick of the first half but it was matched by an excellent piece of goalkeeping from Edwin Van der Sar, who took off to palm the goal-bound effort away.

Pretty tame efforts from Ronaldo and Nani suggested United's early struggle for goals was not going to be confined to the Premiership for the time being. But this emotional night took a turn for the better for Ronaldo and United in the 62nd minute.

In a rare move of sweeping penetration, United dashed forward and Wes Brown delivered a low cross that saw a stooping Ronaldo steer home a header, injecting some much-needed confidence into the Reds' ranks.

Sporting fans lived up to their name and swallowed their disappointment to warmly applaud Ronaldo when his name was read out as a goalscorer on the stadium sound system.

Perhaps the gesture was made because they still believed they could get something out of this game, but they had reckoned without the stunning form of Van der Sar.

He may not have too many campaigns left in which to repeat his '95 European Cup win with Ajax, so this seemed to become a personal crusade for the talented keeper.

Inspired by Ronaldo's goal Nani's performance improved, but it was the veteran Dutchman who overtook Ronaldo as United's main man.

He bettered his flying stop from Liedson by unbelievably keeping out a point-blank header from Tonel with eight minutes to go.

Louis Saha's rustiness stopped the French sub from putting the issue beyond doubt when he screwed a Ronaldo cross wide.

A standing ovation from the Sporting crowd capped a Ronaldo homecoming that had started off colourless but had grown into an evening to remember, although not one to file under his best efforts for United.

Manchester Evening News
September 20, 2007.

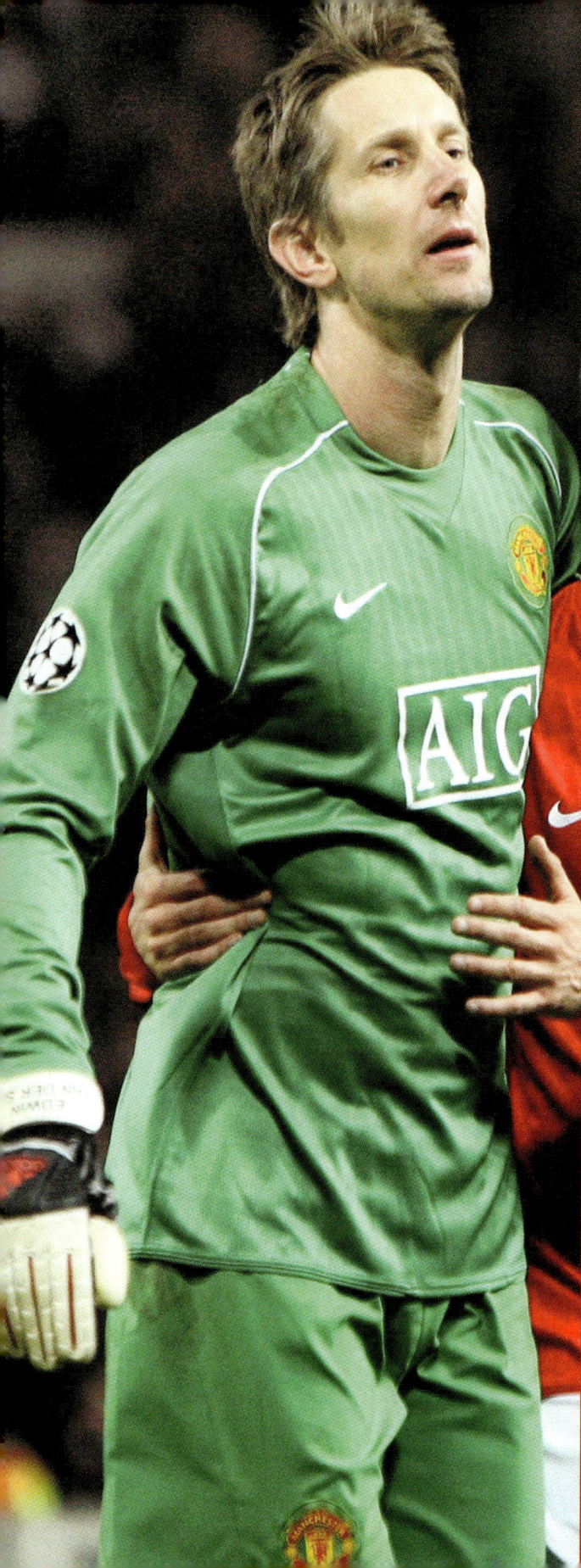

SPORTING LISBON:

Stojkovic; Abel, Tonel, Polga, Ronny (Pereirinha 74); Izmailov (Vukcevic 55), Veloso, Moutinho, Romagnoli (Purovic 67); Djalo, Liedson.
Subs not used: Tiago, Paredes, Farnerud, Gladstone.

UNITED:

Van der Sar; Brown, Ferdinand, Vidic, Evra; Ronaldo (Tevez 85), Carrick, Scholes, Giggs (Anderson 76), Nani; Rooney (Saha 72).
Subs not used: Kuszczak, Pique, J Evans, Eagles.

GROUP F AFTER SPORTING LISBON SEPT 19							
	P	W	D	L	F	A	PTS
AS Roma	1	1	0	0	2	0	3
UNITED	1	1	0	0	1	0	3
Sporting Lisbon	1	0	0	1	0	1	0
Dynamo Kiev	1	0	0	1	0	2	0

Cristiano Ronaldo consigned his former club to a Champions League defeat by scoring in the Jose Alvalade Stadium.

His celebrations were muted after clinching victory for United.

"This is my colour, red, this is my team, but I like Sporting – it's my second home and I am a little bit sad, but Manchester is my team," he told reporters in the post-match mixed zone.

"These people are very important to me. But I am happy for the victory and three points.

"It was a perfect night – I score, I win. It was great for Manchester United.

"It is always important to win away. It was a fantastic game that everyone enjoyed and I think the result was fair."

Sir Alex Ferguson was delighted with the reception Ronaldo received from his ex-fan base in Lisbon, despite the disappointment the Sporting support suffered as a result of the 22-year-old's goal.

"It is very rare in modern-day football that anyone gets a reception like that," said the United boss.

"Obviously, Cristiano is a former player – but it is more than that. I think they recognise they have had an incredible young talent here.

"Sporting helped him through his early development for seven years. Now we are fortunate enough to have him for what we hope will be the best years of his life."

Ferguson also paid tribute to veteran number one Edwin Van der Sar for his part in the opening group success in Portugal.

"Edwin has been with us for three seasons now and when I bought him I thought he was going to be one of my best buys," said the United manager after the match.

"I should have done it years ago when I had the chance but I let it slip through my fingers.

"Even now, at 36, he still has such great enthusiasm. He has played 120 times for Holland and has won everything in the game, yet he still sets such a great example for all our other goalkeepers."

Ryan Giggs believed United's away win was a pointer to an improved European record on their travels and also hailed Dutch keeper Edwin Van der Sar's efforts.

"We hope we are better equipped now to win away matches in the Champions League," he said

"We set about it in the right way. We looked solid. Defensively we were very good. We looked quite good on the counter-attack as well.

"It was just that last pass or last decision that we need to put right. Hopefully the form away from home will get better.

"It was a very important win. You want to get off to a good start in the group stage and we have done that."

Ronaldo's match-winning homecoming may have stolen the headlines but it was United man-of-the-match Van der Sar who was the foundation for the Reds' slim win.

"Edwin didn't put a foot wrong," said Giggs.

"Some of the shots he made look easy by keeping hold of them. He could have quite easily spilled them because the pitch was quite bumpy. The save in the second half from Tonel when he was at full stretch is what wins games for us.

"Edwin has that calming effect and he doesn't make that many mistakes. That's how you gauge a goalkeeper, by the amount of mistakes, because if they do make them then it is a goal.

"Edwin has done it for so long you take it a bit for granted. But top goalkeepers give you a calming influence and that's what you see with our clean sheets."

MANCHESTER UNITED v AS ROMA

PRE-MATCH

United's Euro task against Roma is there in black and white – stop the Italian avengers.

That was the message ahead of Roma's return visit to Old Trafford just seven months after being destroyed in last season's quarter final.

Boss Sir Alex Ferguson was aware the Italian media were whipping up a revenge mission after the 7-1 trouncing dished out by the rampant Reds last April.

And Fergie warned an expectant United crowd to tone down any expectations of a repeat of "perhaps the greatest European night I have experienced at Old Trafford".

The United boss said: "I have bought some of the Italian papers and it is all about revenge.

"It seems the Italian media have only one thing in mind and that is revenge. I think we upset Italian sensibilities and pride when we beat them 7-1.

"Understandably it is a big occasion for them after the defeat they suffered last year. There is a big motivation for them.

"They will want to turn that scoreline round. Even though it was a thrilling occasion for everyone associated with United, I still had to feel for the Roma coach Luciano Spalletti. He must have felt humiliated. He handled it with great dignity.

"Now he has to come here again and handle the emotional part of the game, with the Italian press looking for him to avenge what, for them, was an embarrassing result.

"However, the name of the game is to qualify for the next phase and this will be far more important to the Roma coach than extracting some kind of revenge for what we all know was a freak result.

"It was a one-off. It won't happen again. European football is not that way nowadays. It was an exceptional performance on the night. I think it will be a really difficult game for us.

"That performance, though, captured the essence of United – colourful attacking football full of penetration, flair and fierce finishing.

"The memory of that classic display is a reminder of the elusive form that we are still searching for this season.

"Our form is turning around. All the front players have

been slow to get to their game. That is understandable. Wayne was out with his injury, Tevez missed pre-season. But we are seeing it come together as a team now.

"The goals will come. But right now I would settle for another 1-0 win."

Wayne Rooney is itching to repeat his Italian Job of last April and get off the mark for this campaign. United's hitman had suffered a 17-game Champions League barren spell up to last spring's visit to Rome that had stretched back to his hat-trick debut for the Reds against Fenerbahce.

He ended that bleak run with a goal in the Stadio Olympico and scored four times in three matches inside 20 days against Serie A giants Roma and AC Milan.

The 21-year-old's broken foot this term interrupted his start and the England striker has yet to score in four matches.

"I am desperate to get off the mark,"
said Wayne.

"It has been a disappointing start for myself getting injured. But I am happy to be back playing and have played three games now and hopefully I can start scoring again and help the team win."

Rooney contributed a single strike in the 7-1 massacre of Roma seven months ago.

He believes the Italians will be keen to wipe out that humiliating memory.

"If I was a Roma player I would be delighted as soon as I saw the draw for the groups to have an opportunity to make it right so soon the season after," he added.

"I am sure they will be fired up for this game more than any other after last season. We have to be aware of that and concentrate on our own job and play the way we can.

"I am desperate to win the Champions League having got so close last season, and we didn't play the way we can in Milan. It cost us in the away leg. Hopefully we can get to the final and win it.

"We are more experienced a year on. We have that bit more experience and the players we have brought in will add extra freshness towards the end of the season which we needed last season. It will benefit us."

PREMIERSHIP TOP FOUR PRE ROMA OCT 2							
	P	W	D	L	F	A	PTS
Arsenal	7	6	1	0	16	4	19
UNITED	8	5	2	1	7	2	17
Manchester City	8	5	1	2	11	6	16
Liverpool	7	4	3	0	12	2	15

Four days after opening their Champions League account with a win against Sporting Lisbon, United were plunged into a heavyweight Premiership contest with Chelsea at Old Trafford.

It was Avram Grant's first match as Chelsea boss after Jose Mourinho's departure.

Wayne Rooney and Carlos Tevez played together for the first time and the Argentinian scored his first goal for the Reds.

Ferguson hailed Tevez following the win: "He's a very good player and he will get better. He's a young lad, but he's got a cocky confidence and awareness," he said.

"He's as brave as a lion and tough as nails. He has tremendous qualities and I'm pleased he's off the mark. It will only help him."

United's kids, however, failed to produce the goods in the Carling Cup at home to Coventry City and were knocked out 2-0.

But the seniors got the club back to winning ways with another 1-0 win at St Andrews against Birmingham City with Cristiano Ronaldo again the match winner as he had been in Lisbon.

Ryan Giggs insisted there was no panic at Old Trafford after United's early season dip in form. Having helped his team to battle back to challenge Arsenal at the top with five successive League wins, Giggs reflected:

"Outside the club there might have been a little bit of a panic after those first few matches, but there was none inside.

"The performances were actually quite good, it was only the results that weren't going for us.

"When you look at how experienced the manager is, and also some of the players I suppose, you knew we were capable of going on a decent run, which is what has happened.

"I guess the irony is that up until the Chelsea game, we had not played as well in the matches we have won as we did, certainly against Manchester City, when we created an unbelievable amount of chances but still lost."

SEPTEMBER 26 – UNITED KNOCKED OUT OF CARLING CUP

United have been knocked out of the Carling Cup, after losing 2-0 to Coventry.

"I was absolutely flabbergasted by that performance," said Sir Alex Ferguson.

"I did not expect that at all. I am not interested in giving reasons or mitigating circumstances. It was just a very bad performance.

"We have trumpeted these young lads a lot, so what has happened was a big shock for us all."

SEPTEMBER 30 – EDWIN VAN DER SAR RULED OUT OF ROMA MATCH

Edwin Van der Sar damaged his toe at Birmingham City and has been ruled out of the European clash with Roma.

"Van der Sar has damaged his toe. It is a worry to lose a man of his experience, but Tomasz Kuszczak is very able and we are pleased we've got someone as good as him," said Sir Alex Ferguson.

Manchester Evening News September 27, 2007.

W ell, what did you expect? United had been at pains to warn there would be no repeat of the heady goal fest of last April and had prepared us all with five previous 1-0 wins in the run up to this.

Sir Alex Ferguson described the spring demolition of Roma as one of Old Trafford's greatest European nights.

It was a hard act to follow for a side struggling for inspiration at the moment and, until Wayne Rooney blasted in the winner with 20 minutes to go, this was going to be one of the more forgettable floodlit occasions.

But just as slender wins against Spurs, Sunderland, Everton and Birmingham are now simply three points towards a potential title total, so are similar victories against Sporting Lisbon and Roma just steps towards the ultimate Moscow goal.

Goal avalanches are great but United fans still went away celebrating from this one.

It is to be hoped that Rooney hadn't got a table booked in an Italian restaurant in Manchester following this game because he is unlikely to be a welcome diner having scored five goals against Serie A sides in his last four games against Italian opposition and had spoken of the desire burning inside him to sample Champions League glory this season having had his dreams dashed last May against AC Milan in the San Siro.

His ferociously drilled match winner was enough to dispatch the Romans this time, and showed his determination to make it to Russia in May.

He had been among the scorers on that never-to-be-forgotten evening in April when United's breathtaking destruction of the Italians had seen Michael Carrick, Alan Smith and Rooney devastate Roma after just 18 minutes.

If that was a swift execution, it looked likely this was going to be a slow death if anything.

After the same amount of time had elapsed during this encounter, all the Reds could look back on was a shinned cross by Nani that needed some wicked spin on it before you could have seriously called it a goal chance.

The Portuguese winger was, however, outshining his more illustrious compatriot Cristiano Ronaldo as he attempted to justify his selection ahead of Euro veteran Ryan Giggs.

The 20-year-old supplied some decent crosses as United began to show a touch more adventure but his best assist after 34 minutes was thundered over the bar by Rooney.

Roma only had four survivors from the XI who started the debacle last April and so they weren't exactly damaged goods.

But nobody will have felt the hurt from last spring more acutely than the club's lynchpin Francesco Totti.

He was at the centre of everything the Italians did but most were from long range and, apart from one scary fumble, deputy keeper Tomasz Kuszczak was equal to it.

Carrick had been the Reds' man of the match in the 7-1 destruction, adding two goals to a top-notch performance, and when the ball sat up nicely for him five minutes from half time, Old Trafford also sat up awaiting the breakthrough.

Sadly the midfielder's shot kept rising before it settled in the East Stand.

Totti had taken a back seat following his early surge of inspiration in the first half, but the break revived him and

United were hanging on when Giuly cut in a cross and Totti swooped as Vidic slipped. He fed Aquilani whose shot went wide.

While it was a virtually impossible task splitting the vote for best Reds player last April, Nani was easily becoming United's top performer. He added another tick against his name when his cross after 56 minutes drifted on to the bar.

Aquilani was gaining ground on Totti as Roma's number one, but damaged his ankle when coming close again after 60 minutes and had to quit the action.

While United were able to slice the despondent Roma apart last Easter, this was altogether more like a typical Italian performance of diligent defending.

But just one illegal sight of the ball in the back of their net was enough to put them right off their task.

Seconds after Ronaldo's back-heel goal had been correctly wiped out, Rooney unlocked the door.

Nani was the provider and the England striker swept in the breakthrough off the post.

Roma didn't collapse like a pack of cards this time around and it was a nervous finale for the Reds as they hung on to Rooney's goal, with Ashton-under-Lyne-born Simone Perrotta and sub Esposito both having glorious late chances to exact some revenge for their humiliation seven months ago.

UNITED:

Kuszczak; O'Shea, Ferdinand, Vidic, Evra; Carrick, Scholes, Ronaldo, Nani (Giggs 80); Rooney (Anderson 85), Saha (Tevez 66).
Subs not used: Heaton, Pique, Simpson, Eagles.

AS ROMA:

Curci; Cicinho, Juan, Mexes, Tonetto; De Rossi, Aquilani (Pizarro 61), Giuly (Esposito 80), Perrotta, Mancini (Vucinic 74); Totti.
Subs not used: Sergio, Antunes, Barusso, Brighi.

GROUP F AFTER ROMA OCT 2						
	P	W	D	L	F	A	PTS
UNITED	2	2	0	0	2	0	6
AS Roma	2	1	0	1	4	3	3
Sporting Lisbon	2	1	0	1	2	2	3
Dynamo Kiev	2	0	0	2	1	4	0

Sir Alex Ferguson was satisfied United again won 1-0 to beat Roma.

Wayne Rooney's first-time effort was enough to ensure maximum points from their two Group F games so far against a side they beat 7-1 at Old Trafford last season.

"I'm pleased because they're a good team, it was a good game and a good European night," Ferguson said.

"A bit tactical at times but a good result for us. Rooney's goal was marvellous. It was similar to the one he scored against AC Milan last season.

"It was all about great passing and a great finish."

It was United's sixth 1-0 win in eight matches but Fergie was unconcerned about the trend.

"Sometimes you go through these spells, but it won't last forever," he said.

"If we'd won 5-1 you'd have been criticising the defence for going to pieces!

"The players are all working hard and showing far more experience this season."

Patrice Evra is confident Manchester United have the quality to better last season's Champions League semi-final appearance.

Although the France international was injured when United were crushed by AC Milan in the second-leg of their last-four clash at the San Siro in April, he felt the pain just as acutely.

A beaten finalist with former club Monaco, Evra is desperate to see his name carved among those who have won European club football's greatest prize.

Although they have not hit anything like top form yet, United have already taken a significant stride towards reaching the knock-out phase, opening their Group F campaign with victories over Sporting Lisbon and AS Roma.

"I don't like to make excuses for what happened last year but we did have a lot of injuries," said the full-back.

"This year, we have a strong squad, with a lot of experience and a lot of quality.

"That does not mean you win the Champions League but I am sure we have the ability to do better than last year.

"It is important for us to win it too. Whether it is this year, next year or whenever I don't know, but I have been to the final once and I want to win it."

With Gabriel Heinze sold to Real Madrid, Evra is now firmly established as United's first-choice left-back and 11 hours have elapsed since United last conceded a goal in either the Premiership or Champions League.

"The clean sheet is very good," said Evra.

"I know everyone talks about the four defenders and the goalkeeper but in actual fact, the first defenders are the strikers, so we all deserve credit.

"But I am proud that we don't concede goals. For a defender when you don't concede a goal it is as good as a striker scoring.

"Having said that, it would be easier for us all if we scored more. But I am not worried. That will come in the future."

DYNAMO KIEV v MANCHESTER UNITED

PRE-MATCH

Sir Alex Ferguson believes United's feared treble-winning strike force of Andy Cole and Dwight Yorke has a new challenger coming up on the rails.

The embryonic Wayne Rooney and Carlos Tevez twin threat has the capacity to recreate the devastating firepower of 1999.

In the Ukraine they could begin a United Champions League match for the first time against Dynamo Kiev in the Olympic Stadium – almost nine years to the day since Yorke and Cole began their Euro career as a deadly duo.

The instant chemistry of the Yorke-Cole duo, which started with a 6-2 win against Brondby in 1998, blasted a path to the historic clean sweep with a joint haul of 53 goals.

Trinidad and Tobago international Yorke led the telepathic pairing with 29 goals and England hitman Cole weighed in with 24 strikes.

Yorke was the Champions League joint top-scorer alongside Andrei Shevchenko with eight goals as United's goal machine thundered towards European Cup success.

It was the kind of link-up Old Trafford fans down the years had drooled over with the pre-Munich Tommy Taylor and Dennis Viollet combo.

"The evidence is good at the moment. We are encouraged but they are young players. We hope they develop as a partnership and get better.

"The signs are very good at the moment, that's all I can say, particularly with them being so young."

"There is a test for every player who comes to United, and we always look at that situation. But Carlos Tevez has provided his own answer to that.

"He's been very, very good. We're delighted with his attitude in training and in matches, and I think we were very lucky to get him.

In the '60s Denis Law and Viollett combined to stunning effect before Law hit it off with equal success alongside David Herd.

In the '70s there was Tommy Docherty's exciting mix-and-match front unit of Stuart Pearson, Lou Macari and Jimmy Greenhoff.

But in Fergie's 20-year era as Reds boss, only Cantona and Hughes approached the lethal duo of the Treble season.

However, the United boss reckons he has pieced together another potential firm to rival his goal-getters from '99.

"In Tevez and Rooney we have two exceptionally good players who are a real threat to defenders," he says.

"We've had some fantastic partnerships at the club over the years and most of them took time to develop, apart from Cole and Yorke, who were terrific in their first season together.

"Wayne is only 22, Carlos is 23. They are both young players. Hopefully in three or four years' time we will see something really special from them.

"Both have got great attributes as strikers. Courage, speed, ability to beat men; all the things are there.

"But it's maturity. Once you see that, you see greater authority, better timing. "When that comes, hopefully they'll still be at this club and people will see what really special players they are.

United have a smash and grab raid on their agenda as they take on Dynamo Kiev.

The Reds have stormed to the top of Group F with two wins against Sporting Lisbon and Roma, leaving them four points off manager Sir Alex Ferguson's annual 10-point total to virtually guarantee their passage to the knockout stages of the latest Champions League campaign.

A third victory against Dynamo will give them nine points, leaving United to finish the job two games early when the Ukrainians visit Old Trafford in a fortnight.

It will leave the visit of Sporting Lisbon in November and the trip to Italy to face Roma in December as dead rubbers.

And the Reds boss wants to kill his group rivals off as soon as he can:

"The intention will be for us to win the match, because the rewards are great for us,"
said Fergie.

"We want to get some points from the two games against Dynamo and that would put us in a great position. We see this double header as a real opportunity for us.

"Obviously you get selfish and you want us to win here, with Roma and Lisbon drawing.

"But it doesn't always work that way. The best thing to do is approach your own game with the right attitude and win it, which we'll hopefully do."

Ferguson added: "We expect them to be really positive about the game and have a go.

"We watched their previous two games against Roma and Lisbon and they have some talented players."

MEANWHILE...

PREMIERSHIP TOP FOUR PRE DYNAMO KIEV OCT 23							
	P	W	D	L	F	A	PTS
Arsenal	9	8	1	0	21	6	25
UNITED	10	7	2	1	15	3	23
Manchester City	10	7	1	2	15	7	22
Liverpool	9	5	4	0	16	5	19

United had just two Premiership matches sandwiched between the European tie against Roma at Old Trafford and the trip to the Ukraine to face Dynamo Kiev.

After a series of 1-0 victories and just the one game – against Chelsea – when the team managed to score twice, the Reds' goal machine finally got into top gear.

They beat Wigan at Old Trafford 4-0 and then destroyed Aston Villa at Villa Park 4-1 as Wayne Rooney finally burst into life on the domestic front.

On the negative side, Louis Saha was forced to withdraw from United's bench against Wigan after a knee problem in the warm up and midfielder Michael Carrick was ruled out for six weeks after fracturing his elbow against Roma.

Darren Fletcher also revealed he'd broken his leg playing for Scotland in September after initially believing he'd suffered a knee injury.

Owen Hargreaves continued to suffer with a knee tendonitis problem.

Paul Scholes was ruled out of United's visit to Kiev with a knee complaint. He was to require surgery and didn't appear again after playing against Aston Villa on October 20 for almost three months.

OCTOBER 16 – RYAN GIGGS SIGNS NEW DEAL

Ryan Giggs signs a one-year contract extension at United keeping him at Old Trafford until June 2009.

"I am delighted to have signed for a further season. I am enjoying football more than ever and I hope to carry on playing football for Manchester United for as long as I can.

"The nearer you get to the end you enjoy it as much as you can. When you are 18 and 19 you think it is going to last forever, but obviously it doesn't.

"We have a great team. Winning the Premiership last season was a great buzz for everyone. Hopefully we can do it again.

"Retiring from Wales last May was a big decision and I said at the time I hoped it would prolong my career.

"Already, although it is only a couple of internationals I have missed, I feel I have benefited. I have done really good training during the international breaks. I am feeling the benefits.

"I don't know how long I can go on but I am feeling as fit as ever and I am enjoying it. I want to play for as long as I can."

Ferguson added: "I am absolutely delighted that Ryan has signed for a further season. Ryan Giggs epitomises the word loyalty, he signed here as a 14-year-old school boy and is still with the club 20 years on.

"Apart from his playing ability he has a fantastic demeanour and is a great role model to the younger players. I am sure he will be at the club for a long time to come."

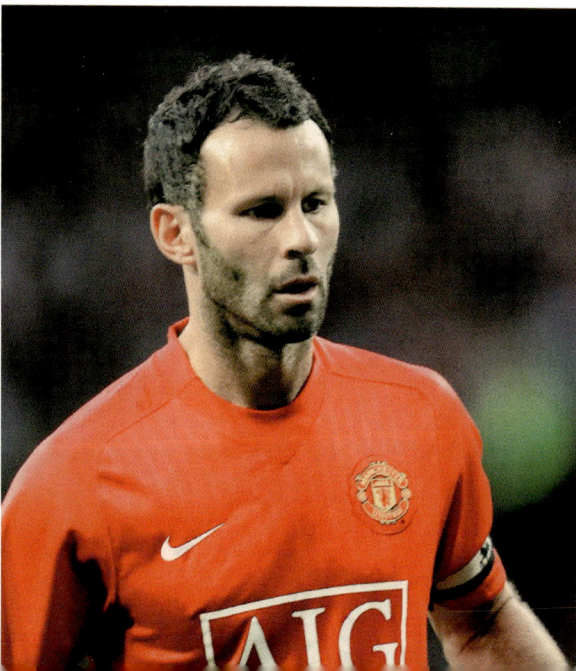

(Rincon 34)	*(Ferdinand 10)*
(Bangoura 78)	*(Rooney 18)*
	(Ronaldo 41)
	(Ronaldo 68 pen)

Sir Alex Ferguson took a nostalgic trip down Memory Lane in his pre-match press conference, recalling the glory days of Dwight Yorke and Andy Cole.

And the Reds took up the theme of those heady Euro evenings in the Treble campaign with this cavalier mix of breathtaking attacks and moments of desperate and sometimes unsuccessful defending to keep you on the edge of your seat.

The 1998-99 golden pairing made their first Champions League start almost nine years ago to the day in Copenhagen when they instantly posted notice of their intent to frighten the pants off Europe with a goal apiece in the 6-2 win against Brondby.

This was United's biggest away win in the tournament since that night of destruction in Denmark. It really was like watching those breathless nights that took United on a crest of an exhilarating wave all the way to their Nou Camp success.

Having ended the 1-0 obsession in the Premiership with four-goal blitzes against Wigan and Aston Villa, United broke up the sequence of replica slim results in the Champions League.

They'd won 1-0 against Sporting Lisbon and Roma in their opening two Group F matches but the Kiev Keystone Cop defence were never in any danger of holding the rampant Reds to such a respectable score.

Paul Scholes' knee injury that struck in training on the eve of this fixture blew a hole in Fergie's engine room.

The United boss believed he'd built a midfield of Euro experience this season, having added Champions League winner Owen Hargreaves in the summer to last term's partnership of Scholes and Michael Carrick.

But Scholes' absence, added to Carrick's broken elbow and Hargreaves' tendonitis problem, emphasised the ill-luck that has beset Fergie's best laid plans leaving an untried combo of John O'Shea and Anderson on the United team sheet sent to UEFA before the match.

However, even that emergency pairing had to be abandoned when Patrice Evra limped off during the warm-up 20 minutes before the game with a calf injury.

It meant O'Shea was switched to left-back and Darren Fletcher promoted from the bench to fill the vacancy in midfield.

Incredibly it meant that United now had only five players from the starting XI that beat Roma at Old Trafford three weeks previous. The Reds have become adept at rising above such a potentially crippling casualty list and once again they shrugged off the latest personnel setbacks with ease.

They would have been encouraged by the Kiev outfit's poor Champions League form. The Ukrainians had failed to win in front of their own fans since November 2004, and picked up just one home point from their group during the previous season.

They were defeated in Kiev in their last European match by Sporting Lisbon, the first game of returning coach Jozsef Szabo, who had replaced their previous boss after defeat in the first Euro match of Group F against Roma.

Clearly the chaos in Kiev has had a more destabilising effect on Dynamo than United's injury curse has had at Old Trafford.

The Reds began repairing a European away record that has suffered extensive damage in recent campaigns with the win in Portugal in September and added to this the reconstruction job in Kiev.

They were in commanding form, with both Rio Ferdinand and Wayne Rooney getting on the scoresheet again, just as they had done at Villa last Saturday.

But it wouldn't be the Reds if they didn't add a bit of drama to the proceedings.

Out of the blue they allowed Dynamo to get a foothold back into the match when a Correa corner after 33 minutes provided Rincon with an unmarked header that neither Edwin Van der Sar nor Cristiano Ronaldo could keep out.

In the 40th minute they restored their commanding look with a third from Ronaldo as he powered in a header from Giggs' free kick.

It became the kind of end-to-end watchable stuff you only tend to witness in the schoolyard, with United digging in to keep a suddenly adventurous and dangerous Kiev at bay and then countering to batter Kiev's defence.

The Reds were never truly in danger of being pegged back and Ronaldo's penalty, after Gavrancic had handled Tevez's cross, chalked up a fourth.

But United's defence, so impenetrable of late, deserted them with Bangoura plundering a second for Kiev in the 78th minute.

Nevertheless, the Reds stride on in Group F.

Manchester Evening News
October 24, 2007.

DYNAMO KIEV:

Shovkovskiy; Ghioane (Belkevich 46), Gavrancic, Yussuf, Diakhate; Gusev, Correa (Rotan 83), Nesmachniy; Bangoura, Rincon, Shatskikh (Milevskiy 46). Subs not used: Rybka, Vaschuk, El Kaddouri, Markovic.

UNITED:

Van der Sar (Kuszczak 80); Brown, Ferdinand, Vidic, O'Shea; Ronaldo, Anderson, Fletcher, Giggs (Simpson 80); Tevez (Nani 73), Rooney. Subs not used: Pique, Evans, Eagles.

GROUP F AFTER DYNAMO KIEV OCT 23						
	P	W	D	L	F	A	PTS
UNITED	3	3	0	0	6	2	9
AS Roma	3	2	0	1	4	2	6
Sporting Lisbon	3	1	0	2	3	4	3
Dynamo Kiev	3	0	0	3	3	8	0

Sir Alex Ferguson is in no doubt United will flourish in Europe after a devastating attacking display in their 4-2 away win at Dynamo Kiev.

United ran into problems in the group phase last season despite matching this year's start with three wins in a row.

But he believes the squad he has now will not make the same mistakes as last term when reverses at the hands of FC Copenhagen and Celtic rocked the Reds.

"Last season we made some changes which didn't work out for us in Copenhagen, then lost to Celtic and we had to win the last game, but this side are more mature now," said Ferguson.

"Our attacking play was excellent in Kiev. We could have scored a lot of goals. Yes, there have been some moments when they were a bigger threat in the second half, but all in all we're very happy with the result.

"All the players are adapting and getting on with it and we're not worried about which formations we're playing or which players because they've all got great ability. We're happy at the moment."

Birthday boy Wayne Rooney is relishing his new partnership with United striker Carlos Tevez.

Rooney, who was 22 the day after the Reds' romp in Kiev, has run into his best form of the season, scoring seven goals in six games for club and country – while Tevez is fast becoming an Old Trafford hit.

"The partnership is really good. Carlos, I thought, was brilliant. His work-rate and his touches were great. We're gelling really well, and I hope that can continue."

Injuries to Patrice Evra and Paul Scholes before the match had disrupted United's planning – but Rooney insists they are strong enough to cope.

"We've got a few injuries at the moment – a lot of key players missing – but we have a good squad and we know we're capable of winning this competition," he said.

"We play Kiev again in a couple of weeks – and if we win we'll be through.

"I hope there's a lot more to come – because after a poor start to the season, we're doing really well."

John O'Shea reckons United have the resources to avoid damage to their trophy aspirations as the injury curse continues to spread through Old Trafford.

Last spring the Reds ran out of steam as the bid for another treble collapsed with first-teamers dropping at an alarming rate.

The blight has not lifted this campaign either, with Paul Scholes (knee) and Patrice Evra (calf) joining the long queue outside the Carrington treatment room.

But the Reds remain Champions League 100-percenters and on the verge of qualification as well as sitting second in the Premiership.

"There is great strength in depth in this squad. That's without a doubt a difference between this squad and previous ones," said O'Shea.

"We're getting stretched to the limits at the minute, but we have some good young lads as well. Hopefully, we'll have some experienced lads back soon but we're showing we can more than cope.

"You'd hope we have the squad to cope with injuries throughout the season now. That's why the manager splashed out in the summer and we'll see the fruits of that towards the end of the season."

MANCHESTER UNITED v DYNAMO KIEV

PRE-MATCH

Sir Alex Ferguson has thrown down the gauntlet to the Reds squad.

Fergie doesn't want the 2008 pool to become 'Nearly Men' and has challenged his troops to win the European Cup:

"If you are one of the best you naturally look to spell it out with cups and medals, otherwise you are in danger of ending your career as a nearly man – and I don't think a single Manchester United player wants that," he said.

"Talk comes cheap but I think we have built a platform that, with just a little bit of luck, will launch us on our way to capture this most elusive of trophies.

"We have had our disappointments on the Champions League trail but, while you can never take anything for granted at this level because the competition is needle sharp, I really believe we are capable of going all the way.

"At this moment in time I am very positive about meeting the demands of this competition this season.

"This team can go far. Certain things have to fall into place, namely to have a good, strong squad by the time you get to March.

"I can't dictate that. It is something you have to accept. You either have injuries at important times or you don't."

Owen Hargreaves is hoping for a European double celebration against Dynamo Kiev.

The former European Cup winner is set to toast his Champions League debut for United and wants to mark the occasion by helping the Reds secure their passport to the knockout stage.

A win for Sir Alex Ferguson's side against the Ukrainians, coupled with Sporting Lisbon failing to take all three points in Portugal against Roma, will see United home with two games to spare.

If Sporting lose, the Reds could afford a draw to book their place in the next stage with the last two games rendered meaningless.

After a 4-2 win in Kiev, Hargreaves is expecting a United win at Old Trafford to be a given.

"They were quite poor over in Kiev," said the midfielder. "In fact I thought they were surprisingly poor for a Champions League team. To concede four goals at home is very rare at that level.

"I am sure they will try better here to redeem themselves a bit but it is a game at Old Trafford for us and we are expected to win it.

"If we do that we should be through to the next round. That will be our goal on Wednesday."

Owen Hargreaves

PREMIERSHIP TOP FOUR PRE DYNAMO KIEV NOV 7							
	P	W	D	L	F	A	PTS
Arsenal	11	8	3	0	24	9	27
UNITED	12	8	3	1	21	6	27
Chelsea	12	7	3	2	18	8	24
Portsmouth	12	6	4	2	23	13	22

Sir Alex Ferguson celebrated his 21st anniversary in charge of United on November 6 and he proved he's still not lost any of his fervour and fury.

Having beaten Middlesbrough 4-1 at Old Trafford, the Reds then went to the Emirates Stadium for the big clash with Arsenal on the eve of Fergie's anniversary celebrations.

United drew 2-2 and referee Howard Webb and Arsenal's stadium security came in for a famous Fergie hairdryer:

"I think Howard Webb has a great chance to be the top referee but today was a big game for him and, at times, he favoured Arsenal," he blasted.

"Their second goal came from him not giving a free kick for a foul on Louis Saha on the far side. It should have been a foul for us.

"It is very difficult for the referee. On our bench, we were getting terrible abuse from people two or three feet away from us.

"There is a lack of security here. It is absolutely disgraceful the abuse you and your staff take. All sorts of things are been shouted and screamed at you and there is an absolute danger here."

Having beaten Middlesbrough 4-1 at Old Trafford, the Reds then went to the Emirates Stadium.

OCTOBER 30 – VAN DER SAR TO RETIRE FROM INTERNATIONAL FOOTBALL

Edwin Van der Sar has announced his retirement from international football with Holland.

"I will stop with the Oranje after Euro 2008 – the time has come," said United's goalkeeper.

OCTOBER 30 – UNITED ANNOUNCE PAUL SCHOLES TO HAVE OPERATION

Paul Scholes has suffered a knee ligament injury.

"He will undergo an operation and will be out for approximately 12 weeks," said a club spokesman.

Scholes suffered the injury during training in the Ukraine before the Champions League match with Dynamo Kiev.

NOVEMBER 2 – GARY NEVILLE MAKES RESERVE COMEBACK

United captain Gary Neville played 57 minutes for the Reds reserves against Stockport County in the Manchester Senior Cup at Northwich.

The right-back has been out since injuring ankle ligaments against Bolton on March 17.

Sadly, plans to include him in the squad to play Dynamo Kiev at Old Trafford were scuppered when the 32-year-old suffered another injury problem.

"Unfortunately, Gary has a little calf strain," said Sir Alex Ferguson.

"It's really bad news for the boy. I don't think it is too bad but it is one he could have done without.

"He needs to get his season on the road and this is a setback."

Sir Alex Ferguson

NOVEMBER 7, 2007
OLD TRAFFORD
GROUP F
UNITED 4 DYNAMO KIEV 0
(Pique 31)
(Tevez 37)
(Rooney 76)
(Ronaldo 88)

United haven't been very good in the past when it comes to anniversary presents for Sir Alex Ferguson, but this was one gift even they couldn't fail to deliver.

In 1996, when the Reds boss marked his tenth year in charge, United went and ruined the festivities by losing at Old Trafford to Chelsea in the Premiership.

Twelve months ago, when he celebrated his second decade at the helm, he was put through misery down at Roots Hall as his side were humiliated by Southend in the Carling Cup.

But after overcoming Dynamo Kiev so comfortably in the Ukraine a fortnight ago, surely they wouldn't mess up the celebrations that had gone on in the week for the Scot's 21st anniversary.

Yet you never know with the Reds, which makes it all the more remarkable that the United chief's health has survived such a roller coaster ride to reach this remarkable landmark.

Whenever you think they've got it easy you can almost bet that they'll slip on a banana skin and make things more complicated.

There was the spectre of last season hanging over this game when the customary picnic was turned into a panic by United.

Having nailed nine points on the board this time last season, the Reds then carelessly lost in Denmark to Copenhagen and then to Celtic in Glasgow.

UNITED:

Van der Sar (Kuszczak 46);
Simpson, Pique (Evans 73),
Vidic, Evra; Ronaldo, Carrick,
Fletcher, Nani; Rooney, Tevez
(Saha 67).
Subs not used: Brown,
Anderson, O'Shea, Eagles.

DYNAMO KIEV:

Shovkovskiy; Markovic,
Diakhate, Fedorov, El Kaddouri;
Ghioane, Vaschuk, Correa;
Gusev (Rebrov 46), Milevskiy
(Bangoura 76), Rotan
(Rincon 46).
Subs not used: Rybka,
Gavrancic, Ninkovic, Dopilka.

GROUP F AFTER DYNAMO KIEV NOV 7

	P	W	D	L	F	A	PTS
UNITED	4	4	0	0	10	2	12
AS Roma	4	2	1	1	6	4	7
Sporting Lisbon	4	1	1	2	5	6	4
Dynamo Kiev	4	0	0	4	3	12	0

Michael Carrick believes competition for places is so great at Old Trafford that manager Sir Alex Ferguson may have a problem picking his first choice XI.

The Champions' investment in the summer on Carlos Tevez, Owen Hargreaves, Nani and Anderson has upped the ante in the senior pool.

Youngsters Gerard Pique and Danny Simpson also impressed against Dynamo Kiev.

Now even £18m England international Carrick is facing a huge fight for a place in the starting XI, having recovered from a broken elbow to return against Arsenal and Kiev.

"The squad is terrific. A few lads have been rested, and that will continue throughout the season," he says.

"The manager has got a lot of bodies, but I'm sure it's a happy problem for him.

"That competition is what this club is all about. They are all top players – and whoever plays will not let anyone down.

"I thought Simmo was brilliant against Kiev and Gerard got the goal so good for him.

"I think everyone has raised their level of performance up a notch or two now, and you can see the threat we have got now going forwards as well as defending a team.

"We are confident we can keep the opposition out and score goals and not lose matches."

After his return to the side, Carrick was just happy to be playing again:

"It was nice to get back. It was a frustrating break, because I was starting to play well and the team was playing well. But it is a long old season, and I am looking forward to the games ahead."

"I don't think it was the perfect performance but it was the perfect result."

Sir Alex Ferguson

THURSDAY NOVEMBER 8, 2007 M.E.N.

64 » SPORT

Sport

manchestereveningnews.co.uk

In association with flybe.com

Hard road
Megson on a Euro mission
» Full story Page 60

Wayne wants the lot

Roo warns Arsenal as Reds seal Euro spot

STUART BRENNAN

WAYNE Rooney helped to fire United into the last 16 of the Champions League – then declared: "Now for the league!"

The Reds striker continued his pursuit of one of Ruud van Nistelrooy's goalscoring records with a goal in the 4-0 demolition of Dynamo Kiev which ensured qualification for the knockout stages.

That means the Reds can now forget about the Champions League until the New Year and concentrate on overtaking Arsenal at the top of the Premier League.

And Rooney said: "We are really confident at the minute, playing some great football over the last few months. We need to keep on doing that and keep up there at the top of the league."

Rooney's strike made it eight goals in his last seven games to keep the Dutch striker's record of netting in ten successive games in his sights, as United eased into the group stages.

But he declared afterwards that he had not enjoyed the match and criticised the Ukrainian outfit for their negative outlook.

"We are delighted to go through, and it means we can rest a few players in the last two group games as we are already in the knockout stage," said Rooney *(above with fellow goalscorer Carlos Tevez)*.

"It was difficult. They came here and were negative. They didn't want to play and that spoilt the game. I didn't really enjoy playing, it was one of those nights, but we did the job and got the win.

"We were frustrated and bored as a team, it was like a training session. They showed no enthusiasm to play the game, so we did a good job."

United boss Sir Alex Ferguson added: "It was a perfect result and gets us into the next stage so we must be very pleased with that. We got a break with the first goal and it opened up the game up for us."

Ferguson hopes the inclusion of rookies such as Gerard Pique, Danny Simpson and Jonny Evans would persuade them to stay at United in the face of interest from elsewhere.

"It shows they have a great chance at this club so they know their future's here."

UEFA CHAMPIONS LEAGUE GROUP F

	P	W	D	L	F	A	Pts
MAN UTD	4	4	0	0	10	2	12
Roma	4	2	1	1	6	4	7
Sporting	4	1	1	2	5	6	4
Dynamo Kiev	4	0	0	4	3	12	0

Eriksson eyeing a January sales bid

CHRIS BAILEY

SVEN-Goran Eriksson can't wait for the Champions League groups to be decided.

And when he finds out – in the middle of December – he will attempt to cherry-pick the best of talent at the clubs who have not quite made the knockout stage.

Eriksson believes that is his best chance to secure players to improve his side.

The Blues boss has been told by owner Thaksin Shinawatra that he will have money to spend on two or three new faces and knows that prising stars from sides involved in the last 16 of the Champions League will be almost impossible.

Instead he will target those who may be feeling the pinch from being knocked out.

It is clear the Swede is not just looking for a striker in the January window, but also some midfield reinforcements.

Michael Johnson's groin problem, that this week needed an operation, has only served to highlight that the side is short on engine-room specialists.

The manager knows that he will have to bring in at least one ball-winner and said: "We are not geared to win the first ball in the air and we are not particularly good at winning the second ball. We do not have that kind of aggressive central midfielder.

"In Johnson and Hamann we have football players, they are not players who will run up and down winning the bits and pieces. So we do not play a game where we move the ball quickly in the air."

Mark Bresciano, Palermo's Aussie international, is one man who might fill that role, especially as it appears Ousmane Dabo is certain to return to Italy in January.

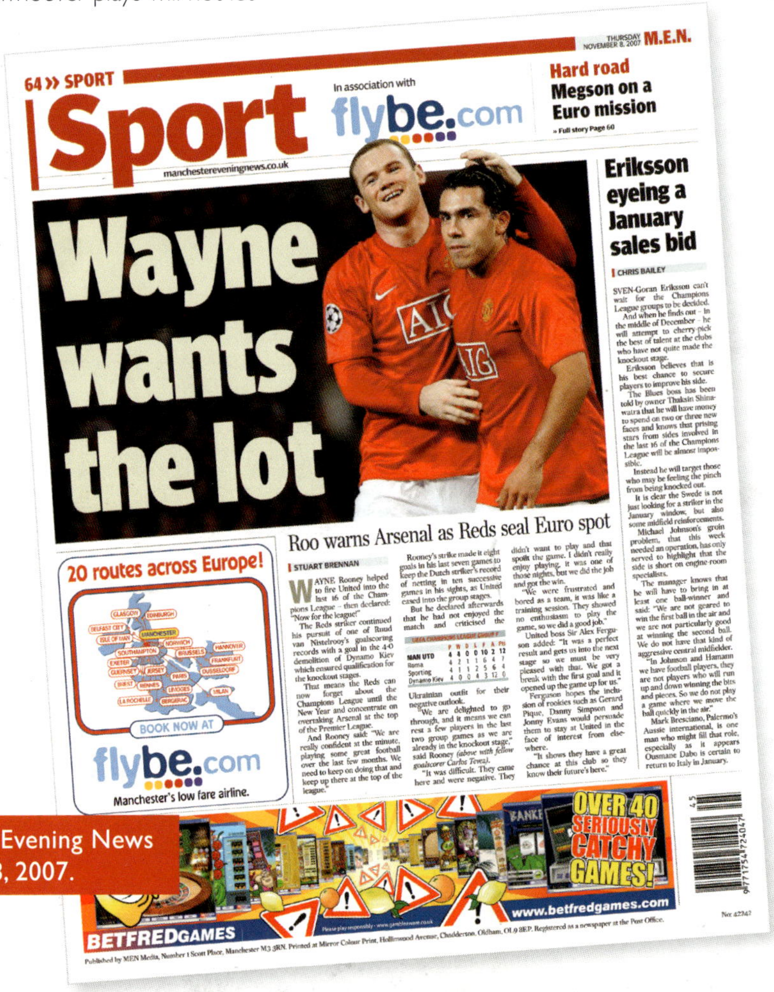

Manchester Evening News November 8, 2007.

MANCHESTER UNITED v SPORTING LISBON

PRE-MATCH

Sir Alex Ferguson is using the top seed card as the carrot for United against Sporting Lisbon.

The Reds are the only side in the Champions League to have maximum points and a win against the Portuguese outfit will guarantee them first place in Group F.

In turn, that placing will see United among the top eight seeds when the draw is made next month for February's knockout stages.

If the standings remain as they are before midweek's matches, it would enable United to avoid the likes of Barcelona, Real Madrid, AC Milan, Inter Milan and Porto in the last 16.

"The incentives are huge for us," said United boss Fergie. "If we win we have won the group and can look forward to being seeded. That is important. Topping the group is a worthwhile target.

"It doesn't always work in your favour but, generally speaking, the fact that the winners of one group will play group runners-up in the next round offers a possible advantage that would be foolish to ignore."

Sporting Lisbon's incentive is even sharper, with Old Trafford's visitors three points behind Group F's second-placed side Roma, with two matches to go.

The Italians are in Kiev to play Dynamo and Lisbon know that three points against the Reds are likely to be a must.

"It is important to keep the winning thread going in Europe," Sir Alex added.

"Winning is a good habit and the last thing I would want to see would be a United team going out with anything but victory on their minds.

"If players don't possess that attitude, the team could easily come unstuck because the Lisbon lads will be buzzing, knowing that if they win their last two matches they'd have ten points and could pip Roma.

"We have to match them because I think they are a better team than their four-point tally might suggest."

PREMIERSHIP TOP FOUR PRE SPORTING LISBON NOV 27						
	P	W	D	L	F	A	PTS
Arsenal	13	10	3	0	29	10	23
UNITED	14	9	3	2	23	7	30
Manchester City	14	9	2	3	18	14	29
Chelsea	14	8	4	2	21	9	28

Mixed fortunes for United in the Premiership. Having beaten Blackburn 2-0 at Old Trafford, they then suffered a 1-0 defeat at Bolton to lose their top spot to Arsenal.

The controversial Reebok match saw Sir Alex Ferguson dismissed to the stands for the second half after a rant at referee Mark Clattenburg at half-time.

"I told the referee what I thought – some referees don't like that. They don't like the truth," he said.

"But I just told him how bad he was in the first half. I know Bolton are battling for their lives at the bottom but they were a bit aggressive and we were looking for some protection from the referee.

"The first half was just a shambles. It was foul after foul after foul.

"I felt they were over-physical and there were two or three really dodgy tackles.

"You hope the referee is strong enough to handle it. But he wasn't."

"Playing in this team is a great privilege," said Serbian defender Vidic.

"This is such a great club and I am delighted to be able to extend my stay here."

NOVEMBER 9 – ROONEY RULED OUT FOR FOUR WEEKS

Wayne Rooney's scoring streak of seven goals for United in seven matches has been brought to an abrupt end.

The England striker damaged ankle ligaments in a game of head tennis at the Reds' Carrington training complex.

"It was an absolute freak accident," reported Sir Alex Ferguson.

"He was playing a game of head tennis and he caught his foot on the stanchion that holds up the net. It's a sickening blow, but we hope he'll be back in four weeks.

"He's been in red-hot form recently, but that's football. He'll miss our games against Blackburn and Bolton – and it's obviously a big loss for England too."

NOVEMBER 13 – UNITED OFFER FANS A ROME EXIT

Violence in Italian football, which led to the football programme in the country being suspended, has forced United to offer their fans the chance to opt out of the trip to Rome in December.

The club are allowing supporters to withdraw their applications up until two weeks before an away European match and will extend the period until 11 days before their last match of the group against Roma.

United will stay in touch with the Foreign Office about their advice on fans travelling to Italy.

A club spokesman said: "For every Champions League game there is a period beforehand where people can cancel. We are not changing our position on the Roma game unless we are advised to do so."

NOVEMBER 23 – O'SHEA COMMITS HIMSELF TO REDS

John O'Shea has signed a three-year contract extension at United that will keep him at Old Trafford until 2012.

"John has developed in his years here and is now regarded as one of the more experienced players," said Sir Alex Ferguson.

"He has proved through his personality and professionalism he is an outstanding credit to the club and I am delighted he has signed a new contract."

NOVEMBER 8 – NEMANJA VIDIC SIGNS NEW OLD TRAFFORD DEAL

Nemanja Vidic has agreed a two-year contract extension that will keep him at United until 2012.

"Nemanja has made a terrific impact at the club and has forged a partnership with Rio Ferdinand that was a major part in us winning the title last year," said manager Sir Alex Ferguson.

"He is an extremely popular member of the squad, both with staff and fans alike. It's great news that he wants to be part of this exciting side for years to come."

UNITED 2 SPORTING LISBON 1

(Tevez 61)   *(Abel 21)*

(Ronaldo 90)

Cristiano Ronaldo saved United once again as they threatened to craft a calamity out of a cruise.

Sir Alex Ferguson had insisted that United's incentive was to win and finish top of the group in order to be in next month's draw as one of the elite seeds.

Maybe he had even reminded his team, and himself, when he was making his selection, that the last time they were strolling in a first-round section they took their foot off the pedal against Fenerbahce in Turkey in 2004 and missed the number one slot.

It meant the Reds ended up being pitched against AC Milan in the first knockout stage and were sent packing.

In Turkey, Fergie had played a shadow side including the likes of Eric Djemba-Djemba, Liam Miller, Kieran Richardson and David Bellion.

Clearly United's underbelly is considerably stronger than the fringe squad who collapsed in Istanbul, but the United manager's assessment that this could be his most powerful pool still has some way to go to proving him spot on.

Without Wayne Rooney, the idea of putting Carlos Tevez on the bench is still a luxury that United cannot fully afford.

Just as in the defeat at Bolton three days previously, when the inspiration of Cristiano Ronaldo was lacking, the Reds certainly need their elite performers.

Ronaldo looked like he fancied putting on a one-man exhibition in the early stages to illustrate just what was missing at the Reebok.

Sporting were driven on by Abel's fluke effort that saw his cross become a goal after 21 minutes, offering them a glimmer of hope in their pursuit of a place in the last 16. But they must have been sickened to arrive in the dressing room at the interval to discover that Roma were 3-0 up in Kiev and likely to be uncatchable.

Not surprisingly, there were victims of United's first half woeful efforts and Nani and Darren Fletcher, from a choice of at least 10, made way for Ryan Giggs and Carlos Tevez to pep up the Reds.

And Fergie's half time masterstroke proved decisive – eventually. The Argentinian's arrival paid dividends but his equaliser was hardly United at their fluent best.

Patrice Evra's 61st-minute burst and cross was touched back by Saha to Ronaldo. The winger miscued and Tevez seemed to know little about his second European goal in two matches for the Reds. Sporting defender Liedson arguably made more contact than the striker!

Scruffy it may have been, but at least it fended off the prospect of a second successive defeat for the Reds.

The wind had been taken out of Sporting's sails by the news from Ukraine and United improved enough to carve out some chances and search for the winner that would ensure a comfortable pre-Christmas outing to Rome.

After the near miss efforts of Owen Hargreaves on free kick duty at Bolton and Ronaldo's limited success from set pieces, it looked like the game would finish as a draw.

Ronaldo was having none of it. He justified his patience and self-belief by steering in the late, late three pointer that saw the Reds top Group F with a 100 per cent record in the section.

UNITED:

Kuszczak; O'Shea, Ferdinand, Vidic, Evra; Fletcher (Giggs 46), Carrick, Anderson, Nani (Tevez 46); Ronaldo, Saha (Hargreaves 79).
Subs not used: Van der Sar, Brown, Pique, Simpson

SPORTING LISBON:

Patricio; Abel, Tonel, Polga, Had; Veloso, Moutinho, Izmailov (Pereirinha 81), Romagnoli (Vukcevic 68); Purovic (Farnerud 80), Liedson.
Subs not used: Tiago, Silva, Gladstone, Paez.

GROUP F AFTER SPORTING LISBON NOV 27							
	P	W	D	L	F	A	PTS
UNITED	5	5	0	0	12	3	15
AS Roma	5	3	1	1	10	5	10
Sporting Lisbon	5	1	1	3	6	8	4
Dynamo Kiev	5	0	0	5	4	19	0

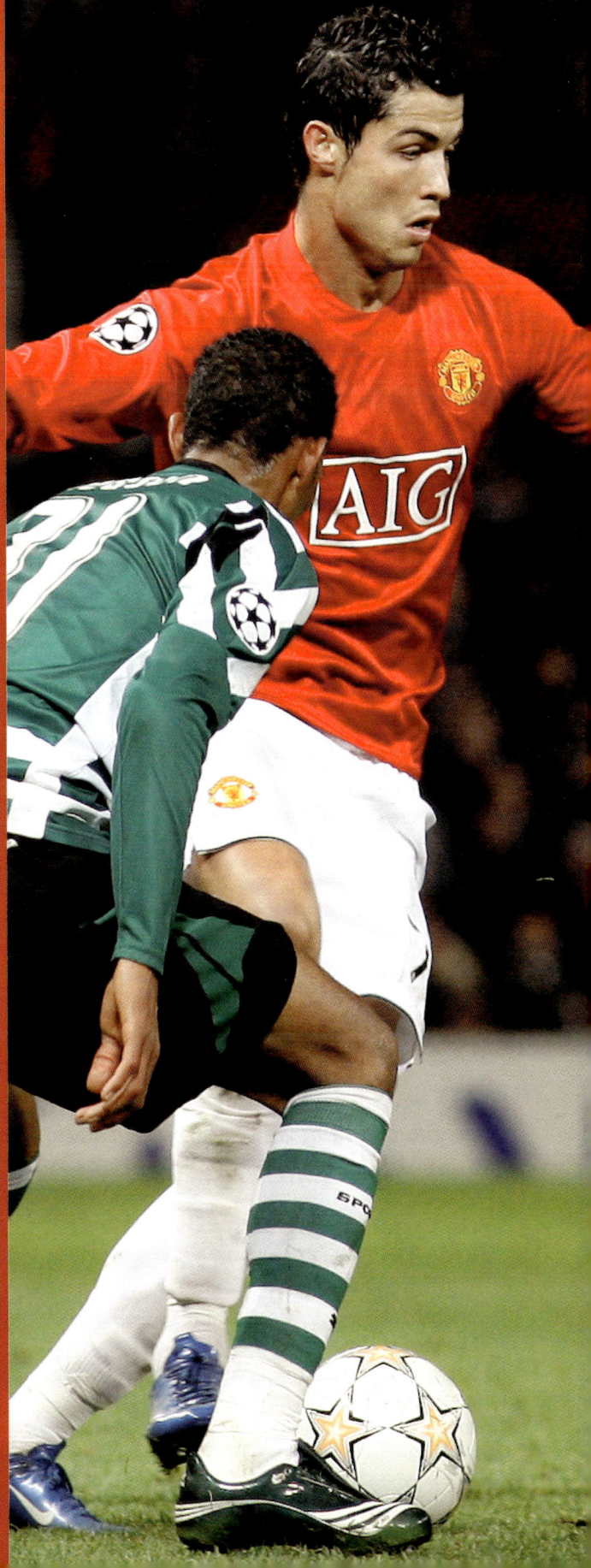

DECEMBER 7 – UNITED SET FOR MID-WINTER BREAK IN SAUDI ARABIA

United are to take up an invitation from HRH Prince Abdullah bin Mosa'ad bin Abdulaziz Al Sa'ud in Saudi Arabia in mid-January.

United will leave immediately after their match at Reading at the Madejski Stadium on January 19, returning before an anticipated appearance in the FA Cup fourth round the following weekend.

They will play an exhibition match against Al Hilal Al Saudi FC in Riyadh on January 21 as part of Sami Al Jaber's testimonial.

"This is a great chance for the players to escape the harsh realities of winter for a few days, while keeping up their fitness levels and taking in the exhibition match," said United boss Sir Alex Ferguson.

"I hope we will come back from this refreshed and ready to continue the challenge for honours."

DECEMBER 7 – UNITED REVEAL MUNICH TRIBUTE

United will create a free, permanent exhibition which tells the story of the Busby Babes as the centrepiece of their plans to mark the 50th anniversary of the Munich Air Disaster which took place on February 6.

The exhibition, to be unveiled in the South Stand tunnel at the stadium, which will be renamed the Munich Tunnel, is designed to educate younger fans about the legendary Babes.

It will chart their early triumphs, through the tragedy of the crash and up to the Reds becoming the first English team to win the European Cup in 1968.

DECEMBER 12 – IMPROVED MEDICAL BULLETIN ON GARY NEVILLE

Gary Neville's bleak medical bulletin has been ripped up by a specialist.

The United captain is back on course for a comeback after he has learned to run naturally again!

"Gary has been to the specialist and it is not as bad as we thought," said Sir Alex Ferguson.

"We think the scar tissue is causing him the problem in his ankle. Maybe it is his running style that's causing it. We are sure it is just scar tissue. It is good news. There is no need for further surgery.

"If he takes the right measures in terms of his running style he will be all right."

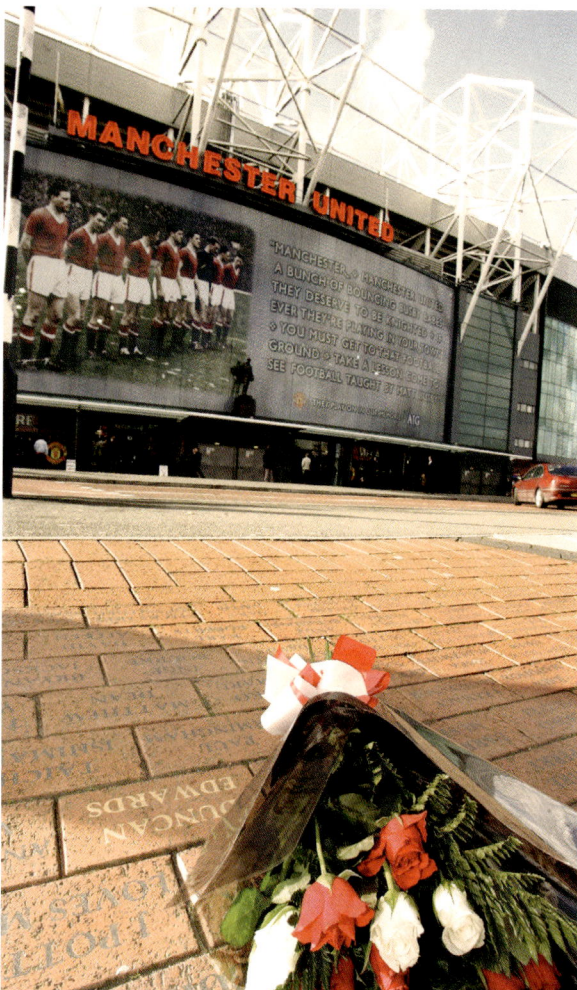

They know a bit about throwing people to the lions in Rome, but United's youngsters didn't get the mauling the locals came to see.

Sadly, neither did the young Reds leave the Eternal City having been able to play their part in a slice of Champions League history.

The honour of joining Barcelona, AC Milan and Spartak Moscow as the only sides with six wins from their six group games since UEFA created the new League from the old European Cup format was denied them by a brief spell of Roma at their most powerful.

Other than that, the curse of previous Euro flops on such otherwise meaningless occasions was successfully avoided, and Sir Alex Ferguson knows for sure now he has some extra names on his squad list who can underpin the strength and quality of the first choices.

There was grim news of stabbings emerging before this match but inside the Stadio Olimpico, where Reds followers suffered so much trauma in April, the atmosphere was flat.

A stadium that generates the most hostile in-your-face mood when it is heaving was only two-thirds full.

It made for a safe environment for United fans once inside the turnstiles but it did nothing to seriously lift this inconsequential match.

It was unlike the cauldron of noise United's shadow squad faced in Istanbul in December 2005 when they collapsed under the strain against Fenerbahce. It scarred players like Eric Djemba-Djemba, David Bellion and Liam Miller and the blemishes on their short and unproductive Old Trafford careers were never erased.

They all ended on a short debit transfer column in Fergie's long reign.

Sir Alex believes the current members of the so-called fringe squad have more about them than some of their predecessors, but it was hard to judge them completely at such a second-gear level of performance by Roma.

Even though coach Luciano Spalletti played a strong XI those home favourites were largely going through the motions.

United's youngsters, with much more to prove, couldn't afford the luxury of strolling through this dead rubber and, against what was put in front of them, you could not fault their application and confidence.

Gerard Pique has had a mixed time in his brief career on the United senior scene.

Though praised by Fergie for his efforts in the shock Carling Cup defeat against Coventry at Old Trafford back in September, it was a judgment by the Reds boss that had many scratching their heads.

Nevertheless, the 20-year-old scored his first United goal against Dynamo Kiev last month but was also at the centre of an alleged but unsubstantiated row with assistant Carlos Queiroz.

Quotes attributed to Fergie's No. 2 claimed the Spaniard wasn't trying hard enough to win his future as a first teamer.

It is hard to imagine there is any truth in that but Pique's up-and-down career in recent months was back on a high in Italy and there could be no complaints about his input.

Not only was he able to cope manfully with the attentions of legendary Roman Francesco Totti, elbows, high studs and all, for the most part, but he also showed again his strength at set pieces with a firm header to convert Nani's 34th-minute corner.

It was probably just what United deserved and it was the Rome crowd who felt the most short-changed.

United continued to show that this exercise would benefit them more than Roma, though some of the home crowd didn't appreciate their favourites' mediocre efforts.

Chris Eagles, Michael Carrick and Louis Saha could all have been celebrating putting the Reds into a more commanding position as United found holes in the Italians' defence easily, with stand-in captain Wayne Rooney to the fore.

But just as the Stadio Olimpico crowd were beginning to turn on their heroes, it was United whose defences were fatally exposed.

After 71 minutes Mancini took on substitute Wes Brown and curled an equaliser home.

Brown again failed to shut down his opponent three minutes later as Vucinic used the space to strike a shot against the foot of the post.

United were now getting a true European test and it was an uncomfortable ending which they managed to survive as the Euro campaign was put to bed for the winter.

AS ROMA:

Doni; Cicinho, Ferrari, Mexes, Barusso (Giuly 62); Esposito (Vucinic 62), Antunes, Taddei, Pizarro, Mancini; Totti.
Subs not used: Julio Sergio, Panucci, Juan, De Rossi, Pit.

UNITED:

Kuszczak; Simpson, Pique, Evans, O'Shea (Brown 54); Eagles, Fletcher, Carrick, Nani; Rooney (Dong 72), Saha.
Subs not used: Heaton, Lee, Hewson, Brandy, Eckersley.

FINAL GROUP F AFTER ROMA DEC 12							
	P	W	D	L	F	A	PTS
UNITED	6	5	1	0	13	4	16
AS Roma	6	3	2	1	11	6	11
Sporting Lisbon	6	2	1	3	9	8	7
Dynamo Kiev	6	0	0	6	4	19	0

Five United fans were stabbed as the Reds latest match against Roma was again marred by violent incidents.

Trouble erupted between 50 rival fans on a bridge near the Stadio Olimpico and police made several baton charges. None of the five stabbed was believed to be seriously injured.

Duncan Drasdo, of the Manchester United Supporters' Trust, said: "I saw several lads in the ground with facial injuries. Some looked quite serious. One, who appeared to have a fractured cheekbone, told us he was crossing the bridge and didn't see what hit him but his friend told him it was a police officer.

"We were sitting outside a café at lunchtime with two lads and were told by their mate when we got into the ground that they'd been stabbed walking across the park. He'd managed to escape but was pretty shaken up."

A United spokesman said, "As a club, we are disappointed that this has occurred as we worked extremely hard with the relevant authorities to avoid any such circumstances.

"Naturally we are concerned for the quick recovery of those involved, but are relieved that the injuries, according to authorities, are 'light'."

United's youngsters won their Euro spurs in Italy despite being unable to steer the Reds to maximum points in Group F.

Old Trafford boss Sir Alex Ferguson had been angered by his fledglings' Carling Cup exit to Coventry in September but was delighted by an improved mature performance in Rome.

The likes of Danny Simpson, Johnny Evans, Gerard Pique and Chris Eagles took the opportunity to prove they can play a part in United's Premier League and European exploits this season.

"I was pleased with a lot," he said. "They gave the ball away too much in the second half, but it was a good performance and we could be pleased with that.

"They lacked experience, but they compensated for that with their ability and played good football against a good Roma side.

"It will help them. The sudden bursts of Roma can catch you out. That's European football and it will do them the world of good."

Gerard Pique has the taste for senior action and is banking on Sir Alex Ferguson feeding his hunger.

The 20-year-old Spaniard hopes his second Champions League goal against Roma on Wednesday, and his successful partnership with Jonny Evans, has sent his boss a reminder that the young duo can underpin the seniors.

"We showed we could play together at Champions League level," said Pique. "Rio and Nemanja are having a great season and are good centre-backs. But it is good for us to show we can play in places such as Rome.

"The squad is strong and we are starting to show that it doesn't matter who is playing – the team is still playing well.

"It is important for us as a group to do that. You always want more and more. Hopefully I will get more games over the rest of the season."

OLYMPIQUE LYONNAIS v MANCHESTER UNITED

PRE-MATCH

Ryan Giggs is set to join an elite band in Lyon when he becomes a member of the Champions League 100 club.

The 34-year-old is in line to stand alongside centurions Raul, Roberto Carlos, Paolo Maldini, David Beckham, Oliver Khan, Luis Figo and Clarence Seedorf.

Manchester Evening News February 20, 2008.

Giggs' European career has spanned 15 years and Sir Alex Ferguson paid tribute to his "model professional". Ferguson said: "There are only a few players who have reached that milestone.

"That is because of Ryan's ability, his longevity and how he prepares – you just have to look at his lifestyle.

"He is obviously at a successful club as well and for me he has been an absolute model in his time with us. Even at 34 we expect big things from him.

"We do not play him in every game but that is natural for someone of his age. It will be a great occasion for Ryan and we are all proud of him.

"When I started in management I wanted to be in this type of competition, playing against the best teams in the world.

"Footballers with real vision think the same way. They have a real purpose in life and want to play in the biggest tournaments.

"Ryan has reserved his best performances for the big occasions.

"When players are asked to be challenged in a big way, it is in European football. You talk about the great nights at Old Trafford and the atmosphere there.

"It can only be because the right type of players are playing on that stage and Ryan has produced many great moments."

Ruthless Reds boss Sir Alex Ferguson will adopt a 'horses for courses' attitude to team selection for United's campaign run-in, and it won't cause him any sleepless nights.

Fergie arguably faces one of his biggest selection dilemmas of the season against Lyon in the Champions League knockout stage.

Apart from injured Gary Neville and Mikael Silvestre, he has his strongest pool to choose from. Darren Fletcher, Nani and Michael Carrick were superb in the FA Cup destruction of Arsenal prior to the visit to France.

But he rested Champions League winners and experienced men Ryan Giggs, Paul Scholes and Owen Hargreaves against the Gunners with the trip to Lyon in mind, and it could be a completely new midfield unit lining up against the French side.

But axing the cup heroes won't be a massive problem to the United manager with his improved squad strength the key to Euro glory.

"Last season we didn't have the resources to get through to the second leg of the semi-final against Milan in Italy," he says.

"If we'd had better resources we'd have got through. But we have a stronger squad and a more complete squad this season. The secret is keeping them all fit.

> *"I am lucky. I have 22 players here and only Gary and Silvestre not here. It is a fantastic position to be in at this time of the season. If we can keep that it will definitely without question give us a chance.*

"The midfield area is where I have the best options. Against Arsenal we brought a couple of fresh players in, in Fletcher and Carrick, and they were outstanding. You could say I have selection headaches. But when you are picking a team at the level we are at, I don't think you look upon that as a hindrance to achieving the result.

"The expectation at our club is that when you are in a tournament you have to do your best. Every game is so important and hopefully we can manage the three."

Wes Brown is out to prove to United he is no longer a fringe player.

The England defender flew with United to France 12 months ago to face Lille as an extra on the Euro stage.

He crosses the Channel for United's latest Champions League test against Lyon as the Reds' regular right-back.

"It is good to be playing week in, week out and hopefully I can keep this going," he said. "You get a routine going. You know what you are doing and know your position."

A year ago the Mancunian was marginalised. He had been displaced in the centre of defence by the impressive Rio Ferdinand and Nemanja Vidic. His other defensive outlet at right-back was sewn up by skipper Gary Neville. But weeks later the captain was KO'd by an ankle injury.

Neville's torment has now dragged on for almost a year as a series of niggles has scuppered all attempts to return on a regular basis.

But since Neville was injured against Bolton in March, Brown has featured in 47 of United's 54 matches.

"In the past I have been in and out of the team after picking up little niggles here and there. This season with the skipper being out I have filled in and am doing OK," said Brown.

"I have been centre-half and right-back and sometimes it is difficult when you are switching week-in, week-out. But I have been right-back all season and this has helped me.

"I have been here ten years so I know what Gary is capable of and what he has achieved for the club.

"For me to fill in for him all season has been perfect for me, but hopefully he will be fit as soon as possible and we will see what happens. All I am doing is playing as well as I can."

PREMIERSHIP TOP FOUR PRE LYON FEB 20							
	P	W	D	L	F	A	PTS
Arsenal	26	19	6	1	54	18	63
UNITED	26	18	4	4	50	14	58
Chelsea	26	16	7	3	38	17	55
Everton	26	14	5	7	41	23	47

United had a roller-coaster ride in winter while the Champions League went into hibernation for two months.

A Merseyside double success against Liverpool and Everton sent the champions into Christmas on a high.

Boxing Day saw them visit old boy and Reds legend Roy Keane at his new HQ up at the Stadium of Light. Never one for sentiment, Fergie's United thrashed his Sunderland side 4-0.

However, the last Premiership match of 2007 ended with a 2-1 defeat at West Ham United and Ronaldo missed a penalty.

United hit back with a 100 per cent January, beating Birmingham, Reading and Portsmouth as well as destroying Newcastle 6-0.

Two rounds of the FA Cup were negotiated with a 2-0 win at Aston Villa and 3-1 at home success against Spurs.

The month ended with Cristiano Ronaldo scoring twice against Portsmouth, with his screaming free kick being hailed by Sir Alex Ferguson as world class quality.

"David Beckham's strike rate was pretty good, Eric Cantona used to take them too, but Ronaldo's strike rate is phenomenal.

"That without doubt must be the best I've seen in the Premier League.

"From that distance he is going to hit them. No keeper in the world would save that. The boy practises. It's a delight to see, terrific."

February opened with United dropping five League points from two matches against Spurs and Manchester City before the Reds travelled to Lyon buoyed by a stunning 4-0 FA Cup fifth round win against Arsenal at Old Trafford.

Defeat against Fergie's men began title rivals Arsenal's slide in the Premiership.

DECEMBER 21 – UNITED AGREE TO SIGN MANUCHO

United agree a deal to snap up Angolan striker Manucho Goncalves.

The 24-year-old has been on trial for the last three weeks at Old Trafford and Sir Alex Ferguson has now handed him a three-year deal, which will come into effect on January 3.

"We have had Manucho here for a three-week trial and have been impressed enough to offer him a three-year contract.

"He is a tall, agile, quick forward and, through contacts that Carlos (Queiroz) has, was brought to our attention around six months ago."

Manucho starred for Angola at the African Nations Cup and was then loaned out to Greek club Panathinaikos.

And the 20-year-old gave a glimpse of why most of French football's luminaries are drooling over the local lad as he crashed a ferocious shot just over, answering United's opening effort seconds later.

Giggs again manufactured a chance for the Reds to complete a two-minute flurry of opportunities at both ends. This time he picked out Scholes but, once again, Coupet proved a stubborn blockade in goal.

Ronaldo finally got going late on in the first-half with a bullet free kick after two previous efforts had smashed into the Lyon wall.

But, yet again, Coupet came up with an answer for United's best efforts.

This might not have been United in full-on cavalier mode as during the Arsenal victory, but nonetheless, as European away matches go, it was calm, and assured and a sprinkling of chances suggested this last-16 knockout stage could be completed with relative ease.

But on European nights, life can switch so quickly from comfortable to calamitous and it was Benzema's brilliance that whipped the rug from under United after 54 minutes.

Rio Ferdinand and Nemanja Vidic had done a more than competent job of restricting the new French wonder talent to one effort, but when he stepped up a gear, the duo simply couldn't contain him.

Benzema controlled a ball from Toulalan with his back to goal, rolled his body and slammed a left-foot shot home with the United pair completely outwitted by the grace and devastation of the France striker.

It was a sign of the changing times at Old Trafford when Nani and Carlos Tevez replaced Euro stalwarts Scholes and Giggs after 65 minutes in an effort to inject some much-needed late impetus.

Having been given the vote for the big occasion, it was sad that the old school failed to ignite the Reds.

The introduction of Tevez to accompany Rooney had the desired effect in shaping a more productive United.

But it looked as though keeper Coupet was going to join Benzema in the hero of the night category for Lyon when he again denied Ronaldo's blistering free kick.

His touch gave United an 87th minute corner and as the Reds piled forward, the French began to panic.

Eventually, it was Tevez who lashed the equaliser into the roof of the net from close-range to rescue the Reds and set up an Old Trafford second-leg decider.

OLYMPIQUE LYONNAIS:

Coupet; Reveillere, Squillaci, Boumsong, Grosso; Clerc (Ben Arfa 78), Juninho (Bodmer 74), Toulalan, Govou, Kallstrom; Benzema (Fred 83).
Subs not used: Vercoutre, Cris, Delgado, Keita.

UNITED:

Van der Sar; Brown, Ferdinand, Vidic, Evra; Ronaldo, Anderson, Hargreaves (Carrick 78), Scholes (Tevez 65), Giggs (Nani 65); Rooney.
Subs not used: Kuszczak, Saha, O'Shea, Fletcher.

United were dazzled in Lyon – but not by the French champions.

A laser beam incident involving United's Cristiano Ronaldo was the subject of a post-match complaint by the Reds in the Stade Gerland

The winger was left dazzled before and during the 1-1 draw by a beam aimed from amongst the French support.

Manager Sir Alex Ferguson said: "We reported the matter to UEFA before the game. We noticed it in the warm-up and UEFA are aware of it."

United went behind to a Karim Benzema superb opener but rallied to return to England with a draw thanks to a Carlos Tevez equaliser.

Fergie was pleased with his team's fight back. He said: "It was a setback to go behind. It was a fantastic goal and it made life difficult for us. But I think we showed our determination to try to get back.

"We lost a goal out of nothing. We were in complete control and it knocked us back a bit. But there was an urgency to get back in the game and I think we are best in that situation.

"They defended very well and made it difficult for us but I think we deserved it without question.

"This has given us a good opportunity to qualify. I don't think Lyon had that many clear chances. Our goalkeeper has not had a save to make and I didn't feel that threatened."

R yan Giggs has started planning for life after hanging up his boots but his short-term objective is helping United into the Champions League last eight.

The 34-year-old, whose Old Trafford contract ends in 2009, will start his coaching badges in Wales this summer.

"Ryan has indicated he wants to come and do his UEFA 'A' Licence with us in Aberystwyth in June," said FA of Wales' technical director Osian Roberts.

"It's great news for us in Wales and I think it's also great news for football that someone of his calibre and status will stay in the game.

"With all his experience and expertise he's going to be a great and valued member to football in the future."

More pressing matters are United's European Cup ambitions.

The late rescue act in France has strengthened their position as favourites to make the Champions League quarter-finals.

"It is a job half done and we will need to play well to beat them at Old Trafford," said Giggs.

"Hopefully, we will finish the job at home. We were happy with the result in the end. Going 1-0 down then to get the away goal so late was good and, hopefully, that will prove a big goal for us.

"It is always important to get the away goals and we got it so we have to be pleased.

"Lyon are a good team and they set their stall out to catch us on the counter and it nearly worked for them.

"They went a goal ahead and weren't really interested in getting the second goal."

Manchester Evening News February 21, 2008.

MANCHESTER UNITED v OLYMPIQUE LYONNAIS

PRE-MATCH

Home rule can be on the agenda for United against Lyon with a place in the record books and the last eight on offer at Old Trafford.

United will equal Juventus's Champions League record of ten straight home wins if they beat the French side.

The Italians set the record in 1997 when the Stadio delle Alpi was the fortress in which Marcello Lippi built the late-1990s success.

Juve's home record saw them to the 1996 and 1997 European Cup finals where they beat Ajax and lost to Borussia Dortmund.

Now Old Trafford can prove to be a similar bastion.

"Our home record in European football has been very good for a long time," says manager Sir Alex Ferguson.

"It has been the foundation for all our group successes in terms of qualifying.

"The atmosphere at Old Trafford on a European night helps. There is a big stimulant for the fans. That has a lot to do with it. The players also like to increase their expectation to do it on a European night.

"This is different to when we played Lyon here before when it was a dead rubber final group match. This is knockout.

"They are capable of getting a goal and we have to be aware that's without question.

"We will be playing attacking football and hopefully that is enough for us to go through."

United certainly have the firepower to crush the French resistance.

Since the low point of 2005, when the Reds failed to qualify for the knockout stages, their run of victories has seen them smash 26 goals in nine matches.

Twelve months ago the focus was on Wayne Rooney and Cristiano Ronaldo's long barren spells in Europe.

But in the last ten matches they've hit back and this season they have scored eight of United's 14 Champions League goals.

"The main reason is they are a year older," said the United manager.

Rio Ferdinand doesn't have the best memory of Moscow's Luzhniki Stadium but he's dreaming of a return visit in May.

The United defender saw the cracks in England's Euro 2008 campaign split wide open in Russia last October in the stadium that will host this season's Champions League Final.

England lost 2-1 and Rio and Co were on their way out of the tournament. But he's desperate to go back on May 21.

"To win the European Cup is the stuff of dreams," said the 29-year-old ahead of the first knockout stage second leg tie against Lyon.

"Any young lad or any professional would say it. Not

many players get the opportunity to play in the final, let alone win it.

"We dream like anybody else to go out there and lift that trophy in Moscow. It would cap off our season if we already have other things in the bag.

"But we wouldn't disrespect our opponents before that by looking that far ahead. It is going to be tough against Lyon. There is a lot of football to be played before anyone thinks about lifting that trophy."

Last April the Reds were 90 minutes from a ticket to Athens for the final but had it ripped from their grasp by AC Milan.

That wound from Italy remains a gaping one.

"Last season we had a good opportunity to go on and be a part of the final. But that didn't happen and we would like to change that," Ferdinand added.

"With the quality we have and the players we've added from last season, we are going to be in with a shout for the trophies we are in at the moment.

"There is a desire in the club to do well in this competition this year."

Since United won the trophy in 1999, Sir Alex Ferguson has several times lamented the fact the club only have two European Cup replicas in the Old Trafford museum.

In the last eight years Real Madrid have won it twice, Milan twice and Barcelona and Bayern Munich have a success each.

It's the name of Porto on the Cup in 2004 and particularly Liverpool in 2005 that irks the Reds' support as well as the Merseysiders' final appearance last term and Arsenal's in 2006.

"We have a great history but would like to be more fruitful in this competition. From the beginning of the season we set our stall out to win every tournament we are in. That is within this club," says Rio.

"If you don't have that mind set at the beginning, you don't deserve to be at this club.

"It doesn't really matter who is in the final or who has been in it before. We have a desire to be there and whoever has played in it before has no bearing on our thoughts.

"Everyone who sets out in this tournament wants to be in the final. Liverpool have done well in the last few years and getting to two finals and well done to them.

"But we look at ourselves and we want to make sure we get through."

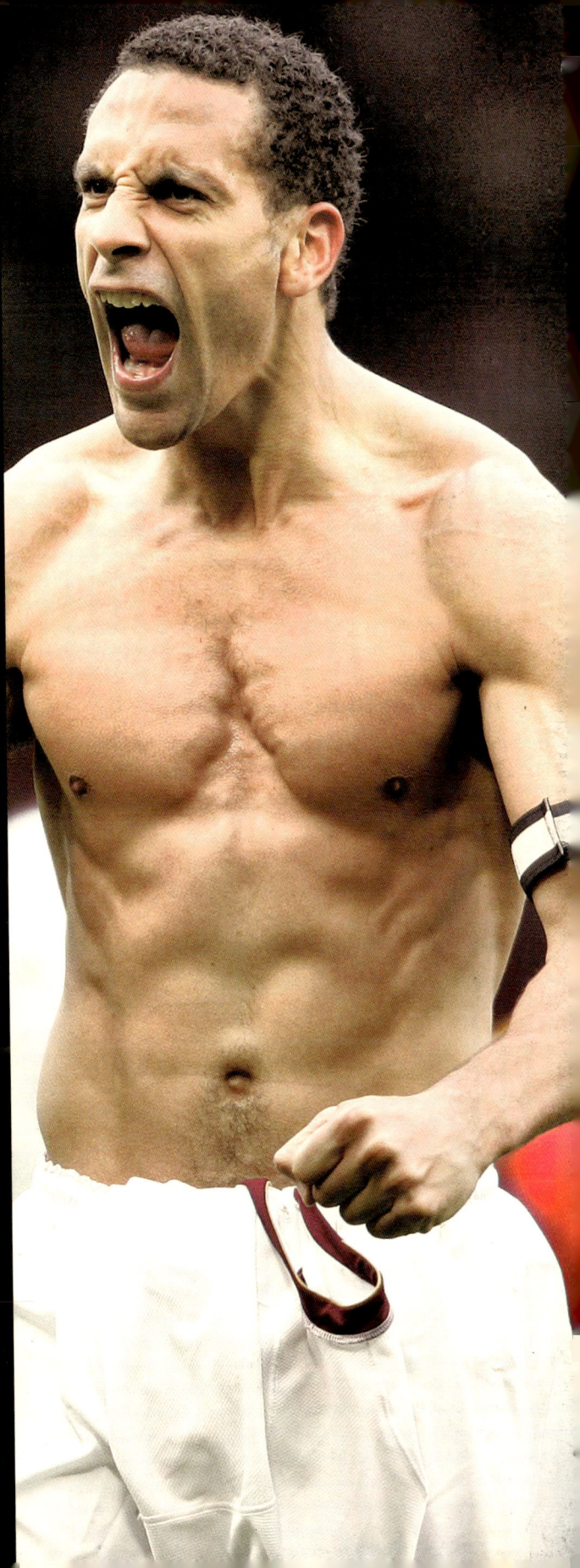

apart and go further," said Rooney after beating Lyon.

"It would be better for English football if we all progress. It would be a shame if we drew each other and two are knocked out.

"Our game has improved so much in the past few seasons. We have proved we have the best league in the world – which is why we attract the best players in the world.

"In my eyes, it is beyond question that we have the best league in the world.

"It is down to English players if they decide to play abroad but for me, English football is the best.

"I love playing here and I'm pretty sure that will never change and that the game will just get better."

The main focus of the rotation policy that has kept the Reds on their toes this campaign has been in a highly competitive midfield department.

But Rooney believes the action is hotting up in United's attack.

"It raises your level, of course, to have competition," added the United striker.

"I see Louis Saha coming back so it makes me determined to play well and stay in the team.

"I don't want to be out of the team. I hated being sub last week at Fulham and I want to play every game.

"But as well as having a lot of match winners, our squad strength is going to be vital.

"At the end of last season we had a lot of injuries and a few tired players but this is a big squad and, hopefully, the rotation policy will help this time around.

"If we get to the last four again, hopefully we'll be a lot fresher because a lot of the players won't have played as many games as they did last season.

"We've brought good players in so the squad is bigger and we haven't got many serious injury problems at the minute. The likes of Anderson and Nani have come in and been brilliant.

"But I think the main thing for our success is that we're enjoying our football. That's a big reason why we're going well in three competitions."

United scraped through the Lyon tie after a below par Old Trafford performance and the 22-year-old hitman says a repeat at the next stage wouldn't be good enough to keep those triple hopes alive.

"If we want to win the Champions League we'll have to improve on the performance against Lyon," he said.

"We got a bit edgy in the second-half, a bit nervous. We're looking for better performances."

AS ROMA v MANCHESTER UNITED

PRE-MATCH

UEFA have threatened to move the 2009 Champions League Final from Rome's Stadio Olimpico if United fans are targeted in the Italian capital.

Ten United fans were stabbed last season when the club played Roma, and there was more trouble when Real Madrid visited last month.

Previously, three Middlesbrough fans were stabbed in 2006 and there have been numerous incidents involving knife-wielding gangs outside the stadium before domestic matches.

The UEFA communications director William Gaillard said they were serious about moving the final if there was more trouble.

Gaillard said: "The situation has improved dramatically and we hope it will go well. There are no reasons to expect problems inside the stadium.

"But we cannot afford to organise the final of the Champions League in a city where people are getting knifed every game.

"We will be watching and we are serious that if we

have incidents like when United visited last year or Real Madrid last month, then we would have to reconsider our decision for the 2009 final."

Paul Scholes is not expecting a free pass to the Champions League Final if United make Moscow – no matter what Sir Alex Ferguson says.

"It is difficult winning the Champions League," the Reds boss added.

> ## "The fact we have only won the European Cup once in my time tells you how difficult it is.

"In that respect it is going to be hard but we have the players who can make us successful, they are confident they can express themselves, they enjoy playing. They are not afraid of challenges and there is enough youth in the team to make them ambitious.

"The one thing these young lads of ours have is the quality to play on the big occasion. They are very confident.

"It gives you hope that they can handle big occasions. You want to see them express themselves and be fearless. I am not even slightly worried about their temperament."

The Reds boss recently revealed a sentimental side to his football character.

Ferguson admitted that because veteran midfielder Scholes missed the 1999 European Cup final triumph in Barcelona because of suspension, he would guarantee him a place in the 2008 showpiece.

But the 33-year-old has dismissed that generosity.

"I think the manager would only play me if I was playing well," said the Salford-born star, who is set to make his 99th Champions League appearance in Rome.

"If I am not playing well then I won't play. It doesn't matter if I missed 1999, it won't make a difference.

> ## "It would mean a lot to play in a final but we have to get past Roma first and through the semi-final. There is a long way to go."

Roma were hit by the news that their legendary striker and skipper Francesco Totti had been ruled out of the quarter-final first leg with a thigh injury.

But coach Luciano Spalletti is confident his side can overcome the absence of Totti and beat a United side he rates as the "best in the world".

Spalletti believes his Serie A high-flyers have enough quality to beat the Barclays Premier League leaders without their talisman.

"Totti is Totti," he said. "But a team that is not able to play without a player does not have the right mentality.

"To have reached this stage of the competition means we have a strong team even without Totti.

"I have a lot of confidence in my players, who I am sure will take on more responsibility as they have done in the past when we have played without Totti."

United goalkeeper Edwin Van der Sar looks set to return to the side against Roma in the Champions League.

Van der Sar was on the flight to Italy after missing the 4-0 Barclays Premier League victory against Aston Villa with a groin injury.

Michael Carrick, Patrice Evra, Rio Ferdinand and Ryan Giggs all travelled after coming off against Villa with knocks.

Mikael Silvestre was a surprise addition to the party after recovering from a knee ligament injury, sustained in September.

However Nani was again missing and ruled out of the quarter-final first-leg match because of a thigh strain.

Ahead of the game Reds boss Sir Alex Ferguson stressed the importance of a clean sheet at the Stadio Olimpico.

With six Premier League matches to go, United have conceded only 15 goals and are bang on course to beating top flight club records of 26 goals conceded in both the 1997-98 and 2004-05 seasons.

They can even beat the all-time fewest goals record of 23 in the 1923-24 Second Division campaign.

And with 20 clean sheets already registered in the League, the defence is close to busting the best ever of 25 in 1924-25 and the top flight record of 26 kept by Peter Schmeichel and Co in 1993-94.

United have also achieved four Champions League shut outs this term. But having conceded one in Rome in December and two last April, United need to shut out the Italians in the Stadio Olimpico.

"Twenty clean sheets in the League is great and I have always said if you defend well, you have a chance of winning things," said Sir Alex Ferguson.

"That will be proved in Rome. If we defend well we have a chance. Roma have improved this season. They are a

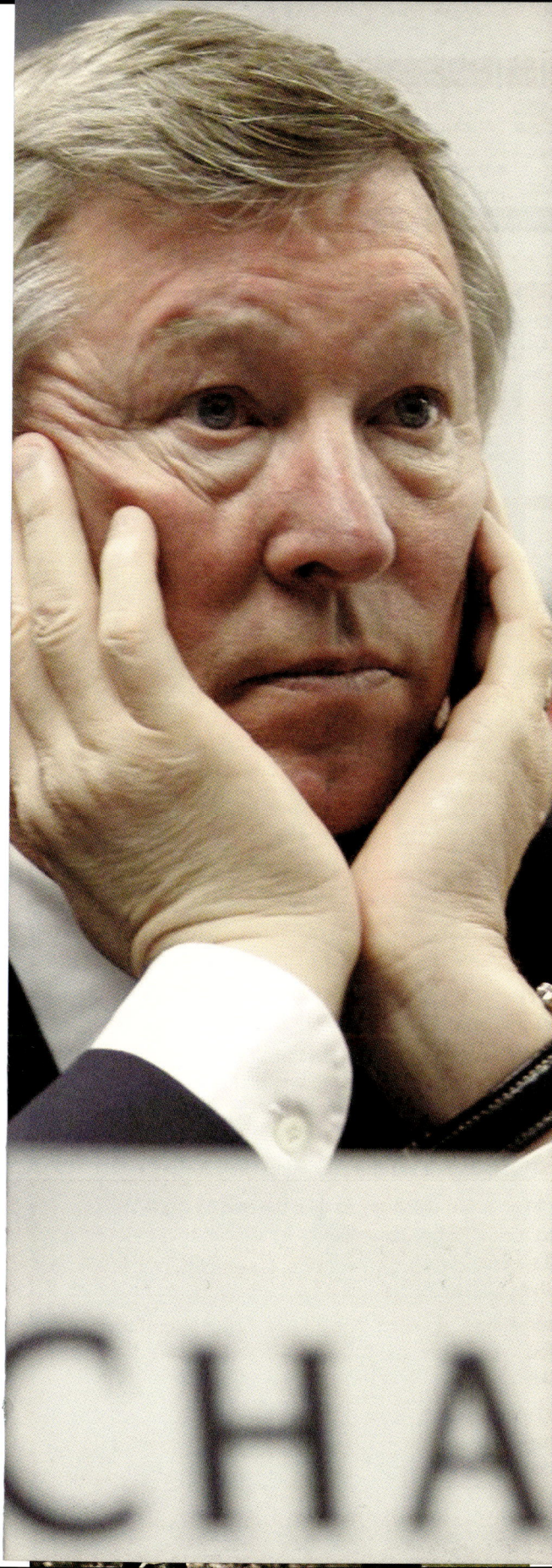

strong team. But we know exactly what we are going to face."

Ferguson knows his side is going into the last eight first-leg tie in the European Cup in high spirits.

"The players reached a peak last week against Liverpool and we continued against Villa," he said.

"They realise now it is a race to the line and we need consistency and real focus. They know they need top level performances and have to play their very best. There has been good evidence of that in the last two games.

"There is great confidence in the way the team is playing. And that is good at this time of year."

United have now got the tactics to overcome Roma's total football and the temperament to bid for the Champions League trophy in Moscow, reckons Sir Alex Ferguson.

The Reds imperiously swept the Romans aside last April at Old Trafford 7-1 to advance to the semi-finals.

But the week before, they came a cropper in Italy, losing 2-1 when coach Luciano Spalletti's game plan threw the Reds into confusion.

During this campaign, United won again at Old Trafford and achieved a draw in Rome at the group stage.

Ferguson is confident his side can cope with Roma's unique strikerless 4-6-0 formation.

"Roma are a job to deal with tactically because they have a different way of playing," said Sir Alex. "But we have faced them four times now so it won't be as big a problem as it was in the first 20 minutes of the first match in Italy last year.

"When you play a team as much as we have played Roma, I wonder who learns the most – the team who has been successful or the team who has lost.

"The only advantage we have is that we have been here twice before. The first time we came here we found it very, very difficult in the first 20 minutes. They press the game very quickly and it took us a long time to adjust to that.

"They are very dynamic, they press forward, and if you lose the ball they counter-attack very strongly.

"Having played them now so many times we hope we have overcome those difficulties."

to be taken. It was just a question of time as to when that breakaway might surface.

With the Romans being quite comfortably subdued, the moment finally arrived after 39 minutes.

United hadn't tested Roma keeper Doni once prior to Wayne Rooney and Scholes laying on Ronaldo's goal.

The keeper never really saw the Portuguese star's thumping header as he suffered the same fate as so many this term watching a Ronaldo effort ripple the netting.

It hadn't all been cause for celebration in the first half as the injury jinx that bit deep into United's resources last spring again blighted the squad.

A year and a day ago Nemanja Vidic had become one of the many run-in casualties at Old Trafford when he dislocated his shoulder against Blackburn Rovers.

It wasn't the sight Sir Alex Ferguson wanted to see again, when the big Serb exited the stage on a stretcher after 29 minutes.

He landed with a jarring thump on his left leg following an aerial battle with Vucinic. Before he'd even hit the floor completely Vidic was signalling a serious problem with his left knee that took the brunt of the landing.

Inevitably there had to be some response from Roma but it was limited. Panucci's 52nd-minute blaze over the bar from a great position ruffled the calm in United's ranks and then Edwin Van der Sar's reflex touch denied Vucinic's header.

The Reds survived and then again proved just what Roma's coach had feared — another devastating counter attack.

Ji-sung Park turned an over-hit Wes Brown cross into an assist as he stretched to send the ball back into the six yard area. Keeper Doni couldn't get his hands round the ball and only finger-tipped it as Rooney struck home.

The Italians were now a spent force and the Reds could easily have made the second leg a definite non-event. Ronaldo struck a post and thrashed a late shot over while Carrick wasted a golden chance.

An even more formidable scoreline would have been a dream but there seems little chance of United not advancing after this clinical performance.

AS ROMA:

Doni; Cassetti, Mexes, Panucci, Tonetto (Cicinho 69); Taddei (Giuly 59), De Rossi, Pizarro, Aquilani (Esposito 77), Mancini; Vucinic.
Subs not used: Curci, Antunes, Ferrari, Brighi.

UNITED:

Van der Sar; Brown, Ferdinand, Vidic (O'Shea 31), Evra; Ronaldo, Carrick, Scholes, Anderson (Hargreaves 55), Park; Rooney (Tevez 84).
Subs not used: Kuszczak, Giggs, Pique, Silvestre.

Cristiano Ronaldo wants to swap armchair admiration of United's 1999 stars for the Champions League winners' podium in Moscow.

In 49 days the tournament's leading goalscorer hopes to be the TV star who will inspire future generations of Reds.

Ronaldo has spent the last five years watching re-runs of United's European Cup success in Barcelona and dreaming of replicating the Nou Camp triumph. Now he aims to turn the dreams into reality.

"I have watched the 1999 final many, many times on television. It is something I want to do as well," he said after United's victory in Rome.

"It is a great competition and, therefore, such a great experience to win it. Every one of the lads wants to win not just the Champions League but also the Premier League.

"And we know we have a good chance, because we are in such a good position at the moment.

"This is a fantastic club with great players. We have the experience. We have the team.

"The lads know that if we carry on like this, we have a good chance to win the Champions League. But we have to take it game to game and, if we do that, we will be OK.

"I think the team improves every year. In fact, at the moment the team is brilliant. Everyone is confident. We are playing nice football and with such maturity.

"If we carry on like we did in Rome, with the next game at home and at 2-0, we have a great situation.

"Maybe we are the best team at the moment. But, we must not forget you have Arsenal, Liverpool, Chelsea and Barcelona.

"Even so, we are in a very good position right now.

"To win 2-0 at a big club like Roma is a very, very good result. It is amazing to go home with that kind of result behind you.

"But it is not good if we think it is all over. We have a great chance but we still have to play well at Old Trafford."

Ronaldo was still sat in front of his armchair on his return from Italy – this time watching his goal against Roma.

The 23-year-old put United ahead in the first half with a thumping header, but was flattened in the process.

"I don't know much about the goal because I went down injured and was in pain so I didn't enjoy it.

"I will watch it again but the lads have told me it was brilliant," he added.

Reds boss Sir Alex Ferguson insisted the Rome victory was far from comfortable, despite the scoreline.

"It's a very good team we played against," he said. "We had to defend really well at times. We had some lucky breaks in the second half – they could have scored a couple.

"We didn't lose a goal, which was really vital. It's a fantastic scoreline for us and I'm very, very pleased."

The one concern for United was an injury to Nemanja Vidic, who was substituted in the first half.

"It's a knee injury," Ferguson revealed. "We're just praying it's not anything other than a nerve injury."

Manchester Evening News
April 2, 2008.

MANCHESTER UNITED v AS ROMA

PRE-MATCH

S ir Alex Ferguson is hoping he can go to bed after the Roma clash and begin dreaming about Champions League success in Moscow.

Not until he is tucked up at home in Wilmslow with a semi-final date secured will he consider the chances of lifting his second European Cup.

Those fantasies about May 21 will stay locked away until United complete the quarter-final task against the Serie A side at Old Trafford.

The Reds lead 2-0 from the first leg in Italy, and no team in Champions League history has ever lost by that scoreline at home in a first leg knockout match and overturned the result to go through.

United also have the considerable psychological boost of having demolished the Romans 7-1 in Manchester last April.

But Fergie is well versed in the shocks that can hit you from left field on such occasions.

"It is our best chance of getting to a semi-final, that goes without saying," he says. "And if we get there then like all the other three teams you can start thinking about the final because you have to have that ambition and hope.

"The sensible approach is to wait until after the game then hopefully we can start to dream.

"We are not looking to do anything silly. There are 90 minutes and that clock keeps ticking away and the clock is against Roma. They have to do something, which may suit us in actual fact because on the counter attack we are very good. Both teams will have their moments and hopefully ours will be enough to take us into the semi-final.

"Having been involved in games against Roma on five other occasions in the last year and knowing how Luciano Spalletti has coached his team, I think they will play their normal game.

"I don't think they will change anything in terms of their approach. They will start in their normal fashion.

"We are aware of the dangers in their team and hopefully we can counter those dangers. The most important thing when you are at home is to express in your performance in a big way.

"Our big hope is we can get the first goal. That takes the pressure off us. It then gives a bigger problem to Roma.

"Knowing my team we will try to do that and attack the best way we can. In a situation like this we do have leeway but we never take anything for granted and won't be doing now. We will look on this match as the most important game of the season for us.

"Let's be sensible about it. We have one foot in the semi-final. To get two feet into the semi the best way is to approach the game in the proper fashion and go and win it.

"We cannot look on the performance in Rome as an absolute pass into the semi-final. We got there because we worked our socks off, because the team discipline was good, because tactically we were very good on the night and that is the kind of performance we need again. It is not an absolute certainty."

United are favourites to win the trophy in Russia and are odds on to dismiss Roma.

Barcelona are also red-hot favourites to beat Schalke in the other last-eight game in the Reds' half of the draw. The Spaniards hold a 1-0 lead from the game in Germany.

That will send the Nou Camp side and United into a last four collision with experts claiming the Reds are the best side left in the tournament.

But Ferguson won't accept the pundits are correct just yet.

"I watch games in Europe and we see different types of football and that makes it difficult to assess where our position is," Sir Alex added.

"The best way for me to assess it is if we are to get to the final. That is the only way.

"At the moment you can be the best team in football and lose. Hopefully that is not the case, but it can happen. That's why we are not in the FA Cup Final.

"Hopefully by the law of averages our performances mean something and we can produce performances that get us to the final.

"It won't be easy. If we get by this one we have a difficult one, probably against Barcelona. They are a marvellous club and good football team. These things are never easy."

Sir Alex Ferguson has hailed Wayne Rooney's forfeit in Rome last week that helped United to the brink of a European Cup semi-final berth.

The 22-year-old was instructed to play in a disciplined left wing role in Italy.

He had to forego the front role he enjoys, but keeping to the game plan in the Stadio Olimpico enabled United to keep their shape and allowed Cristiano Ronaldo a more destructive central role.

It added up to one of United's best tactical away displays for years as they won 2-0, with Rooney even managing to add to Ronaldo's goal.

Fergie was delighted with his attitude in Rome.

"It was a demonstration last week of personal sacrifice for the sake of the team effort," said Sir Alex. "He sacrificed his own normal role in the team to work for the side. It was a great demonstration of a great player.

"He is only 21. With anyone of that age you are waiting for the completion of his potential and I think that will happen in the next two or three years."

PREMIERSHIP TOP FOUR PRE ROMA APRIL 9							
	P	W	D	L	F	A	PTS
UNITED	33	24	5	4	70	17	77
Chelsea	33	22	8	3	58	23	74
Arsenal	33	20	11	2	63	27	71
Liverpool	33	17	12	4	57	25	63

With just nine days between United's quarter-final ties with Roma, the Reds were able to just squeeze one Premiership match in – but it blew the title race open again.

There was April snow at the Riverside as Middlesbrough held the champions to at 2-2 draw and even more bad news came when Rio Ferdinand put himself in doubt for the Roma clash at Old Trafford when he injured his left foot.

Wayne Rooney rescued the Reds on Teesside with 16 minutes to go.

But goalkeeper Edwin Van der Sar was still backing United's makeshift back four to see the Reds through their defensive crisis and over the line in the title race.

"Nemanja Vidic is a very important player for us but it was just a coincidence that conceding twice against Middlesbrough came while he was absent," said the Dutchman.

"It is better to play games with the same formation but I have no doubts about the players we have. Wes Brown and John O'Shea, for instance, can do it for us.

"A draw was not going to be that bad at Middlesbrough, but losing was out of the question.

"We have to get at least a three-point difference between Chelsea and us before we go down there to Stamford Bridge.

"It is going to be very tight. It is still a three-horse race. Arsenal will come on Sunday and they will want to beat us.

"Chelsea don't have an easy programme so it is not to say they are going to win all their remaining matches."

APRIL 3 – VIDIC OUT WITH KNEE INJURY

A scan on the knee Nemanja Vidic injured in Rome has revealed a brighter picture for the Serbian.

The Reds' centre half landed awkwardly in the Champions League quarter final first leg clash in the Stadio Olimpico causing concern at Old Trafford.

But a United statement said: "There is no major damage to the left knee, and he will be out for two to three weeks."

Sir Alex Ferguson said: "Of course he is a loss but I think we can cope.

"If we cannot, there is something wrong. We are very well covered in his position."

APRIL 6 – GARY NEVILLE RETURNS TO FIRST TEAM SQUAD

Old Trafford skipper Gary Neville is finally back in contention for a place in the senior squad having not played for the first team since March 2007.

"It has been a long road back for Gary," said Fergie.

"He played a full match for the reserves this week, which was good. His personality and experience will help us.

"It is not easy at his age but his enthusiasm for the game and his determination to get back, that is what gives you the most encouragement about him. I think he will figure in some games this season."

APRIL 9, 2008
QUARTER-FINAL
SECOND LEG
OLD TRAFFORD
UNITED 1 AS ROMA 0
(Tevez 70)

The dream is now on! Sir Alex Ferguson was adamant he wouldn't think about Moscow until the Italian job was done but surely he would have had sweet dreams as he dropped off in his Wilmslow bed fantasising about a trip to Russia.

United are heading back to the scene of his finest hour, or perhaps three minutes, as Barcelona stand between the Reds and their first Champions League Final since the Nou Camp in '99.

The Class of 2008 will be in the Catalan capital for the first leg of the last-four clash. And it would be an ironic travesty if the club that has dominated the Premier League since its inception in 1992 was unable to set up the first ever all-English final to showcase the domestic elite division in Moscow on May 21.

Old Trafford's PA system belted out the Barcelona anthem at the final whistle, one that brings back so many memories of the countdown to the final nine years ago.

There is the same sense of destiny around the stadium now as there was in the build-up to those magnificent ten days that concluded the Treble.

Fergie and the fans have suffered so many European disappointments and near misses since that glorious Spanish evening, but this was surely not going to be one of them.

Nevertheless, it wouldn't have been the Reds had they not made it through without a touch of drama to spice up what could otherwise have been a mundane occasion.

United had not gone into a knock-out second leg match in a more commanding position since hosting Deportivo La Coruna in April 2002.

Six years ago the Reds returned from Spain with a 2-0 lead courtesy of Ruud van Nistelrooy and David Beckham goals in La Coruna.

There were to be no shocks at Old Trafford that night, even though the second leg 3-2 scoreline suggested a more troubled game than anticipated.

But on that evening United had made it 3-0 on aggregate before Deportivo managed to claw a goal back and they didn't score their second until the 90th minute.

This was an even more comfortable situation in that there was also the immense mental plus of having torn the Italians apart last spring 7-1.

October's 1-0 group win against Luciano Spalletti's side did, of course, temper any feelings that another memorable destruction could be on the cards, but surely the unforgettable avalanche a year ago would mean something.

The task for the visitors was to score three goals at Old Trafford and no team has done that since Chelsea in May 2005, and nobody has ever managed it without reply in the Champions League. Even two goals in 120 minutes without the Reds scoring and then a penalty shoot-out was surely a mission impossible.

But there is always that little niggle in the back of your mind where the Reds are concerned; they do have this minor streak in their nature to set the nerves jangling in matches where there should be no issue whatsoever.

Fergie also adds to that slight uncertainty at times.

It's easier to land the 1-2-3 in the Grand National these days than it is to guess Sir Alex's starting line-ups.

As firmly planted as one of United's boots was in the

semi-final, you would not have gambled your Aintree winnings on Rio Ferdinand playing and Wayne Rooney and Cristiano Ronaldo beginning the night on the bench.

And as for Paul Scholes sitting alongside them, well...

As much as the Reds boss has confounded all those this term who've questioned his sanity when they've seen certain line ups, it was always a half-hearted snigger at his expense.

The last time he had the last laugh when leaving Rooney and Ronaldo in the dugout was at Fulham at the beginning of March when United still won 3-0.

The days seem to have passed when opponents have looked at a United team before a match and felt so disrespected it fired them up for revenge.

Unbelievably there were only five survivors from the Reds XI that thrashed the Italians last April, and in an even bigger show of squad strength there were only two players, Rio Ferdinand and Michael Carrick, who started the group match against Roma at Old Trafford in October!

For their part, the Serie A side retained eight players who had been savaged at Old Trafford 12 months ago, and it was just 11 minutes before they'd shipped the first goal back then.

The battle for biggest roar of the night contested between Roma's missed penalty, Eric Cantona's half-time welcome and Tevez's winner, was finally won by Gary Neville as he came on as a substitute with nine minutes remaining for his first senior match in 13 months.

The midfield role was unfamiliar and certainly a one-to-one aerial challenge on keeper Doni was definitely unusual, but a tackle on Vucinic and the sight of the captain's armband on his arm was much more familiar.

UNITED:

Van der Sar; Brown, Ferdinand, Pique, Silvestre; Park, Carrick (O'Shea 74), Hargreaves, Anderson (Neville 81), Giggs (Rooney 74); Tevez.
Subs not used: Kuszczak, Ronaldo, Scholes, Welbeck.

ROMA:

Doni; Panucci, Mexes, Juan, Cassetti (Tonetto 56); De Rossi, Pizarro (Giuly 69), Taddei (Esposito 81), Perrotta; Mancini, Vucinic.
Subs not used: Curci, Cicinho, Aquilani, Brighi.

Sir Alex Ferguson set his sights on European glory after United booked a Champions League semi-final showdown with Barcelona.

Carlos Tevez scored the decisive goal in the 74th minute to seal a 1-0 quarter-final second leg win over Roma with a diving header to help the Reds cruise through and set up a glamorous meeting with Barca.

Earlier Daniele De Rossi had missed a penalty for Roma after Wes Brown brought down Mancini inside the box, but Ferguson felt the referee made a mistake to award the spot kick.

Fergie said: "It was the wrong decision for the penalty – I thought Wes had got the ball. The penalty miss made a big difference.

"I said before the game that both teams would have their moments in the game, and for the first 25 minutes of the game we were on top. Their goalkeeper made some good saves."

Fergie still has painful memories of a 4-0 defeat in the Nou Camp in 1994. But he insists his side are much better prepared for Barca this time around after booking their place in the last four with a 1-0 win against Roma last night.

He said: "We probably got an early education against Barcelona. We drew with them at Old Trafford and then lost 4-0 at a time when you were only allowed three foreign players and I made one of my great decisions to leave out Peter Schmeichel which didn't turn out well."

But Ferguson has much happier memories of the last time he faced Barca when United drew twice with them on the way to the Treble in 1999.

The sides drew 3-3 at Old Trafford and then again by the same score in Spain in two of United's most memorable matches in Europe.

And Fergie is expecting another thriller: "Both teams represent the way the game should be carried out,"

"Both tried to play attacking football.

"I look forward to going up against them with what is a very good team."

Gary Neville made his long-awaited return to action for the final nine minutes of the clash with Roma – and was just happy to be there.

The Reds skipper slotted into midfield after more than a year of injury problems and said: "I hope for this season I can come in and play a small part because it's frustrating missing run-ins.

"I got a good reception. Constantly over the last 12 months people have been asking me 'when are you coming back' and it can get a bit embarrassing at times.

"The fans have always been great to me and they were tonight. Now we've two unbelievable games of football to look forward to – two football clubs who play the game the right way and they will be unbelievable occasions to be part of."

"Anyone who is a football fan will be tuning in."

BARCELONA v MANCHESTER UNITED

PRE-MATCH

Sir Alex Ferguson is demanding the spirit of Turin '99 surfaces in the Nou Camp when they meet Barcelona in the first leg of the Champions League semi-final.

The Reds boss insists his side have the "bottle" to stun Barcelona and write their own successful chapter in the Old Trafford history books.

The Catalan outfit have a 100 per cent home record this term in the Champions League, with ten goals scored and only one conceded in the tournament.

Nine years ago Fergie's side went to Italy to face Juventus whose Stadio delle Alpi form was equally formidable.

United suffered a catastrophic opening in Turin and were trailing 2-0 after 11 minutes.

But Roy Keane inspired a fight back that saw the Reds storm to the final.

"The Juventus semi-final in 1999 was without doubt our best ever performance in Europe," says Sir Alex.

"That is exactly what we need now in Barcelona. Juventus was an examination of that side's character and their bottle.

"They went 2-0 down and then went at them and ended up winning well.

"This is exactly the same situation now. We are facing a side whose European record at home is very, very good.

"And it will be a massive pitch which will help Barcelona retain the ball."

The United boss believes United have the personnel to replicate Keane and Co's glory night.

"You look at the form of Michael Carrick and Anderson and how they have developed," he added.

"Wayne Rooney and Cristiano Ronaldo are as good as the players we had in 1999. They play without fear.

"They know it is a semi-final and you can't win without

Manchester Evening News April 23, 2008.

showing your true mettle. We were not ready for last season's game against AC Milan in the semi-final but I am far more confident now."

Despite the Turin history lesson, Ferguson doesn't want his current squad to be bombarded by the ghosts of Barcelona '99.

"That was almost ten years ago. This is a team for today," he said.

"They don't need to worry about the past or be reminded of the past. They have seen it on video many times.

"But more important is that they can shape themselves and make their own history. They are good enough to do that.

"Manchester United and Barcelona must be among the strongest sides in Europe as they have come to this stage of the competition.

"Both clubs deserve to be there and this match would be an attractive final, a fantastic occasion.

"I believe the winners of this game have a great chance in the final."

Sir Alex Ferguson

United must improve on a poor Champions League semi-final record to overcome Barcelona.

In Sir Alex Ferguson's previous 12 campaigns for the European Cup, the Reds have only been successful in one last four encounter – against Juventus in 1999.

The first blemish of that unenviable record came against Borussia Dortmund in 1997, while in 2002 Bayer Leverkusen upset the form book to dump the Reds at the last hurdle.

Then, 12 months ago, AC Milan wrecked United's final ambitions.

"It is about raising the bar, " said Sir Alex. "We have had challenges in European football and sometimes we have failed them. I think last season we were undone by circumstances in Milan, but the previous time in Milan we failed badly in the last 16.

"We have failed in some semi-finals when we should have won. Leverkusen and Dortmund are two we should have won.

"We need a raising of the bar. We need more concentration and a better retention of the ball, definitely.

"I think we deserve to be here. Our performances have

been good, no question about that. The Roma and Lyon performances were good – as you know their European record has been good over the years so we have come through well to this point.

"Hopefully, we can score the goals that matter and take them back to Old Trafford without the worry of not having scored.

"If we get a goal, it gives us a massive advantage."

The Reds had injury concerns going into the Nou Camp test.

Wayne Rooney had injured his hip against Blackburn in the Premiership and was forced off at Ewood Park.

Then in Barcelona Nemanja Vidic missed the hour-long training session in the stadium on the eve of the match and was later rushed to a Spanish hospital with a stomach complaint.

The Serbian defender had been present at United's pre-match press conference in Barcelona but felt unwell afterwards.

He remained in hospital for two hours before being discharged and returning to United's hotel.

Michael Carrick is happy to let Barcelona do all the worrying ahead of United's Champions League semi-final clash.

Lionel Messi has been passed fit and both Thierry Henry and Samuel Eto'o are fired up to reach Moscow. Though Ronaldinho has been ruled out of the game, Barca still have the quality to reach the final.

"It will be a test but I would like to think it will be more of a test for them and how they cope with us," said Carrick.

"If we can get a goal or two, it would be a really big boost coming back to Old Trafford.

"As a footballer, it does not get much better. The way we both play our football sets it up as the perfect game to watch.

"It promises to be a great spectacle, and obviously everyone is talking about it because you dream about being involved on a night like this at the Nou Camp.

"Manchester United have not been there for a while but the lads who were around in 1999 have spoken about what a special night it was. Hopefully we can repeat some of that success."

BARCELONA:
Valdes; Zambrotta, Marquez, Milito, Abidal; Deco (Henry 77), Toure, Xavi; Messi (Krkic 62), Eto'o, Iniesta.
Subs not used: Pinto, Gudjohnsen, Silvinho, Giovani, Thuram.

UNITED:
Van der Sar; Hargreaves, Ferdinand, Brown, Evra; Rooney (Nani 76), Carrick, Scholes, Park, Ronaldo; Tevez (Giggs 85).
Subs not used: Kuszczak, Anderson, Pique, O'Shea, Silvestre.

Cristiano Ronaldo insisted he will have no hesitation in stepping up to the plate the next time United are awarded a penalty despite his second-minute spot kick blunder in the Nou Camp.

"Next time I get a penalty, I will try and put things right. I am not scared," he declared.

"I am always confident. I have 38 goals this season. It is not a problem if I miss one or two. I try to do my best in every game.

"Since I have been in Manchester I have scored 15 or 16 penalties, I think, and missed two. "No-one has said anything to me because I always try to score, to play well."

Owen Hargreaves, who performed heroically as an emergency right-back, said: "Cristiano has scored more than he has missed, so it is fine what happened.

"Maybe he should have had another penalty. But that was always going to be a difficult decision for the referee.

"He had already given one early in the game and we were the away team."

The contentious incident occurred in the 30th minute when Ronaldo was bundled over by Rafael Marquez but Swiss referee Massimo Busacca did not give the foul.

"While you have to respect the decision of the referee, he did not make the best decisions," added the Reds' winger.

"Too many decisions went to Barcelona. He gave us nothing."

But he was convinced United's firepower would rise to the occasion in the second leg at Old Trafford.

"It wasn't the best game in Barcelona but in Manchester we will try to win," he said.

"I'm sure the return game will be totally different. Barcelona won't keep the ball like they did in this match and we'll create more chances.

"It will be a different game and I'm sure we're going to play better. We are at home; we will have 75,000 people behind us. We will try to play good football and try to win."

Hargreaves, too, was anticipating an improved United showing back in Manchester to set up the first all-English

Champions League Final in Moscow against either Liverpool or Chelsea.

"We are optimistic as we will play a lot differently than we did at the Nou Camp," said Hargreaves.

"We will attack Barcelona and see how they deal with it.

"They had a lot of possession but did not really penetrate us. We had a strategy and played really well."

Rio Ferdinand left the Nou Camp knowing United's credentials were on the line in the second leg.

"If we lose against Barcelona in the second leg everyone will say we're not as good as people are saying," he said.

"If we win we'll get the plaudits we deserve, if we don't we'll get the criticism we probably deserve.

"But we'll never be over confident. I'm sure the stage is set for a fantastic tie. If you were a betting man it wouldn't be easy to put your money on anyone. We know that.

"The tie is not over. They're a very good passing side, if you're not focused for the whole 90 minutes and concentrating that whole time, then I'm sure they'll find the gaps to score goals.

"But in the Nou Camp I thought every one of us defended resolutely. Getting the news that Nemanja Vidic was ill was a big disappointment because he has been fantastic this season.

"But I think it speaks volumes for the squad that Wes Brown came in and played centre half and Owen Hargreaves played right back and to keep a clean sheet under those circumstances against one of the most potent attacking forces in European football was very pleasing."

As for Cristiano Ronaldo's penalty miss, Ferdinand added: "You can forgive him that because he's had such a great season and has been there when we needed him.

"No one has any hard feelings, nothing was said. He's had ups and downs so I'm sure this is just another page in his story."

MANCHESTER UNITED v BARCELONA

PRE-MATCH

Proud Sir Alex Ferguson has put his trust in the troops that he believes will fire United into the Champions League Final.

The 0-0 stalemate in the semi-final first leg at the Nou Camp has left the Reds needing to win against Barcelona at Old Trafford if they are to land their third European Cup success in Moscow.

United's attacking verve deserted them in Spain, but Fergie is positive his team will rediscover their firepower in front of their own fans and book their final place in the Russian capital.

The Reds boss said at an Old Trafford pre-match press conference: "I thought our performance in the first leg was probably our poorest in Europe this season, and naturally that's a worry as you look for reasons to explain why our attacking skills deserted us.

"However, I remain confident we can come out on top. I know we can play a lot better and will do so. We won't make the same mistakes.

"The players are well aware they under-performed in certain areas and I know they are determined to put things right. They won't let anyone down. I am sure of that.

"I trust these players. I am happy for them to represent United in any shape or form and in any game no matter.

"I am a lucky manager to have such good lads. Character-wise they are fantastic. You saw that in the second half at Chelsea. It was magnificent.

"I am absolutely proud I have these players representing myself and the club tonight.

"I think Barcelona know it will be a different United. That won't be lost on them. It is a difficult game coming to Old Trafford. That won't be lost on them either, especially Thierry Henry who will know what to expect after playing so many times in Manchester.

Manchester Evening News April 29, 2008.

Juventus in 1999, Bayer Leverkusen in 2002 and AC Milan 12 months ago.

And the 34-year-old's only pre-match message to his team-mates is: "Enjoy it."

"First and foremost the players have to go out and enjoy it," Giggs said.

"It is the semi-final of a European Cup at Old Trafford. You have to enjoy these games. This is why you become a footballer.

"Then it is a case of do what you do best. If you defend then you defend. If your game is attacking and taking on players and try to score goals then do that.

"But most of all go out and enjoy it. These games don't come around too often. You have to make the most of it. I am sure we will.

"Every player is looking forward to it. It is a massive game and we will be up for it."

Giggs certainly won't be attempting to dampen the spirits of the younger element of the Reds squad.

"The enthusiasm is what these sort of players bring to the team. You are not going to calm them down," Giggs added.

"That is why we have been so successful this season because of the youthful enthusiasm they have got. "It has been infectious. It has carried through the team. We have a good mix of youth and experience.

"The experienced players use their experience. We have players who have played in European Cup finals before and players who have nearly got there like last season who want to get there. The younger players bring their enthusiasm. I am not going to calm them down. If they perform to the best of their ability, which they have been doing all season, we'll be OK."

Giggs said the Reds would have to rekindle some of their attacking flair to KO Barca.

"We defended brilliantly against a very good team in Spain" he said.

"But we could have created more. But with the Old Trafford crowd behind us we are noted for our attacking play. We score and create chances; that is what we hope we will be doing.

"Obviously you don't neglect what we did at the Nou Camp and that was defend as a team, defend as individuals and stop Barcelona from creating chances. We have to defend like we did but create more chances and I am sure we will."

"It will be more open than at the Nou Camp and it could go either way but I am confident."

United have the back up of an 11-match unbeaten home run in Europe that is now the best Champions League record.

"We have a great home record. It is marvellous. It surpasses any other team in Europe and we are proud of it," said the United boss.

"But it doesn't change the aspect of the game. It will be balanced and open. It will be tactical at times but there will be times when there will be explosions of play that we expect from our team.

"The home record doesn't matter, it is just a good record that's all, but the fans can make an impact."

European Cup winner Ryan Giggs urged his United mates to revel in the big-match Old Trafford atmosphere against Barcelona.

Giggs, a veteran of 102 Champions League matches, has seen experienced do-or-die semi-final second-leg missions before – against Borussia Dortmund in 1997,

PREMIERSHIP TOP FOUR PRE BARCELONA APRIL 29							
	P	W	D	L	F	A	PTS
UNITED	36	25	6	5	74	21	81
Chelsea	36	24	9	3	62	25	81
Arsenal	35	21	11	3	66	29	74
Liverpool	36	19	13	4	64	28	70

A heavyweight title bout was the meaty filling in the Barca butty as United's double bid gathered pace.

But the brakes were put on early celebrations by Chelsea as the Londoners beat United 2-1 at Stamford Bridge.

A win would have all but ensured the Premiership trophy remained at Old Trafford.

But a controversial game and after match in the capital left the title still in the balance.

Sir Alex Ferguson rounded on referee Alan Wiley after the 2-1 defeat.

The United manager was furious that a penalty was awarded against Michael Carrick with four minutes

remaining, which Michael Ballack converted to put Chelsea level on points with the Reds.

Wayne Rooney looked to have rescued a point after he cancelled out the opener from the German midfielder, but Ballack had the final word, leaving Ferguson questioning whether Chelsea should have ever been given the penalty.

"It was absolutely diabolical," he said. "It is a major decision. Granted, it hit his hand. But he has not lifted his hand above his shoulders, above his head, anything like that.

"It is going straight to Rio Ferdinand. The referee should have seen that rather than the linesman. If we're not going to get those decisions then we are under pressure and we're going to have to perform really well.

Ferguson maintains United are still in the driving seat – given their superior goal difference – with two games remaining.

"It's still in our hands," Sir Alex said. "The players and the support are really fired up for the next game. Hopefully we can get the result we want."

Following the match, a group of United substitutes were involved in a post-match bust up with Chelsea groundstaff during a warm-down session at Stamford Bridge.

Patrice Evra, Paul Scholes, John O'Shea, Gerard Pique and Gary Neville were on the pitch when they were asked to move.

The row erupted when the players refused to come off the pitch and an altercation broke out between Chelsea stewards, groundstaff and the United players.

APRIL 26 – INJURIES HIT UNITED FRONT AND BACK

Wayne Rooney aggravated a hip injury scoring United's equaliser against Chelsea and Nemanja Vidic lost a tooth and needed stitches after being accidentally kneed in the face by Didier Drogba at Stamford Bridge.

Both are doubtful for the Old Trafford Euro tie against Barcelona.

APRIL 26 – BALLACK SAYS UNITED ARE FEELING THE HEAT

Chelsea's Michael Ballack says United are under pressure as they prepare for the title two-match finale.

Ballack's two goals enabled the London side to draw level on points with the Reds and erode a five-point lead.

The German was a member of the table-topping Bayer Leverkusen side eight years ago that eventually lost the title on the final day to Bayern Munich.

"In 2000 I was in a similar situation at Leverkusen, but we were the ones leading and Bayern Munich caught us," said Ballack. "In the last game we were three points in front, but lost the game and the title.

"It can happen up to the last minute. The pressure is on them because last week they looked like they were the champions. They had a five-point lead and now we have closed the gap.

"Manchester United still have everything in their hands but the pressure is on them. It looked like they were champions, but now it's getting smaller and tighter."

APRIL 27 – RONALDO IS VOTED THE PLAYERS' PLAYER OF THE YEAR

Cristiano Ronaldo has been named as the Professional Footballers' Association player of the year.

United's goalscoring winger wins the award for the second successive season.

"I feel very happy. It is a great moment; it is an honour, a pleasure," said the Portuguese star.

Ronaldo beat off competition from Liverpool duo Fernando Torres and Steven Gerrard, Cesc Fabregas, Gunners team-mate Emmanuel Adebayor and Portsmouth goalkeeper David James.

Ronaldo did not attend the event, as he was busy preparing for United's Champions League semi-final second leg clash with Barcelona, but said: "When you work all season to play good, to do something for the team, and then at the end of the season the PFA give you this award, it is a great motivation to carry on like that, to work more and get better.

"I feel very good but it is not just my award, my team-mates have helped me a lot this season. It is a good moment for me."

APRIL 29, 2008
SEMI-FINAL
SECOND LEG
OLD TRAFFORD
UNITED 1 BARCELONA 0
(Scholes 14)

Paul Scholes and ten others in the Champions League Final it is then.

Sir Alex Ferguson promised the Salford-born star he would be in his team for Moscow if United made it to their third European Cup final.

The midfielder later poured cold water on the offer, saying he would have to be playing well to take that guarantee seriously.

Well, surely now he would have to be playing like a drain not to have secured his position in the line up at Luzhniki Stadium on May 21 after firing the Reds into the final for the first time since 1999.

Scholes was afforded that rare Fergie promise because of his Turin torment in '99, when a yellow card cost him a place in the Nou Camp against Bayern Munich alongside his pals from the Class of '92.

It is often difficult to know how the poker-faced Scholes is feeling. His face as he walked off the pitch at the end of his glory evening at Old Trafford last night did not look too much different to his look in the Stadio delle Alpi nine years ago!

But after all those agonising years following his Juventus heartbreak, Scholes finally ended his European misery and United's long wait with a glorious 14th-minute winner.

It was a night of unbearable tension, but unless you could have brought Roy Keane out of retirement for this one occasion, nobody deserved to be the hero more than Scholes.

The weight of history does not seem to have bothered United, as they have been reminded all campaign of the desire to honour the 50th anniversary of Munich, plus the 40th anniversary of the first European Cup success, by winning the trophy again.

But history was against the Reds. It would have been wise for Fergie to have banned papers, TV sets and internet access for his players in the run up to this game as there was a thick pile of stats being peddled around to worry the Reds.

United had never reached a European Cup final via a second leg at Old Trafford; their success rate after goalless draws in the first leg was a paltry 25 per cent; and when they have failed to score in the first leg, they had previously been knocked out.

Even if Sir Alex had successfully kept that depressing list of bad omens away from his troops, they would know that Wayne Rooney has been absent for five of the Reds' seven defeats this campaign. Rooney had aggravated his hip injury scoring the equaliser at Chelsea when he was gifted a pass by Ricardo Carvalho.

Obviously Barcelona had not been scrutinising the DVD of the Bridge encounter as their defender Gianluca Zambrotta committed the same crime by setting up Scholes after 14 minutes.

If there is anyone you would want to have a clear shot laid on from 25 yards then it would be the Ginger Prince,

UNITED:

Van der Sar; Hargreaves, Ferdinand, Brown, Evra (Silvestre 90); Nani (Giggs 76), Carrick, Scholes (Fletcher 76), Park, Ronaldo; Tevez.
Subs not used: Kuszczak, O'Shea, Anderson, Welbeck.

BARCELONA:

Valdes; Zambrotta, Puyol, Milito, Abidal; Messi, Xavi, Toure (Gudjohnsen 88); Deco, Iniesta (Henry 60), Eto'o (Bojan 71).
Subs not used: Pinto, Edmilson, Silvinho, Thuram.

one of the sweetest and hardest strikers of a ball the club has ever had. He lived up to his reputation with a curling effort that Valdes had little chance of stopping.

It settled United down as they had looked edgy up to the opener, and not surprisingly as Barca's key man Lionel Messi was clearly in the mood for a trip to Moscow.

If ever he gets fed up walking down Las Ramblas, United should break the bank to see if he fancies Market Street!

The only high drama in Spain in the first leg came after just 94 seconds when United were awarded their penalty for a handball. A good minute was stripped off that blockbusting start when Scholes whipped Messi off his feet close to the edge of the penalty area.

Referee Herbert Fandel called it correctly, much to the Reds relief.

After the opening blitz of action in the Nou Camp, the first leg became a dull affair that did not belong amongst the previous epic encounters these two sides have given us down the years.

Last night the cloak of negativity was thrown off by United, and Barca were every bit as impressive on the eye, as they had been in Catalonia.

With both Edwin Van der Sar and his opposite number Valdes looking like accidents waiting to happen, and both defences seesawing between desperate and dynamic, this was always going to be an edge of your seat thriller to make up for the Nou Camp bore.

Every fan who sat through that deserved this as repayment.

Nani and Ji-sung Park had good chances to put the Reds further into the lead in the first half while Barca's two best attempts at an answer both came from Deco.

As an attacking force, the Reds were contained in the second half apart from one early Carlos Tevez shot, and Old Trafford became increasingly fidgety as Barcelona, inspired by Messi, pressed and pressed. Had they a cutting edge then United would have been in trouble.

Caught up in the anxiety of knowing a single Barca reply might spell curtains, the crowd dared only muster one half-hearted rendition of *United are going to Moscow*.

It was an excruciating finale as the match went into injury time, but then the travel plans to Russia began in earnest.

MANCHESTER UNITED v CHELSEA

PRE-MATCH

Sir Alex Ferguson is convinced fate is United's 12th man in Moscow and will be steering the Reds towards European Cup glory.

Destiny has played a huge part in the Reds' European glory.

In 1968, ten years after the Munich air disaster, survivor Bobby Charlton scored twice at Wembley and captained the Reds to European Cup success.

Another survivor, Bill Foulkes, scored only his second United goal of a long Reds career to seal United's passage to that final with a goal in the Bernabeu against Real Madrid.

In 1999 United beat Bayern Munich in Barcelona on what would have been Sir Matt Busby's 90th birthday.

This season Paul Scholes, who missed the '99 final through suspension, scored United's semi-final winner against Barca.

This year, of course, has seen the 50th anniversary commemorations of the Munich tragedy.

European success this term has been seen as a fitting and emotional tribute to the Busby Babes who were killed in Germany.

United manager Fergie confessed in February that the

burden of honouring the Babes made him nervous. But the Premiership title success has eased the load:

"Now we've got there I feel more relaxed,"
he said.

"I think winning the league makes you more relaxed. We're going there with good momentum and good confidence. I've got everyone fit and I couldn't be going into it in a better frame of mind.

"Fate does play its part. It's a strange thing to discuss because you wouldn't think such a thing was possible.

"But there have been so many coincidences. The Sunday we won the title, for instance, was 25 years since Aberdeen won the Cup Winners' Cup.

"May 11 is a good day for me and I felt quite confident about that – though I did have to suffer a bit at Wigan.

"And you know another strange thing? It threw it down on both occasions. Think about that."

Chelsea's XI in the Luzhniki is set to overshadow United's final choice in terms of experience.

But Ferguson is convinced his young guns will relish the Moscow stage.

"People ask do they have the experience to take opportunities like this," added Sir Alex.

"But young people aren't afraid. That's the great quality young people have.

"When I was a kid I used to climb steeples of churches looking for pigeons and go under bridges and all the rest of it. Now, if I look outside a window more than two storeys high I get vertigo.

"That's what age does to you. When you're young you are fearless. So, hopefully the younger ones in the team will be like that.

"I wouldn't expect my players to freeze."

United's Moscow XI is picked but it will remain stored in Sir Alex Ferguson's head until the chosen few are revealed publicly before the final.

The next task is to choose the moment to delight eleven players, offer seven the solace of a place on the Luzhniki bench and break the bad news to seven more that they'll stay in their suits for the Champions League Final.

But Fergie has again pleaded with UEFA to reconsider the numbers on the bench for future finals.

"It is not easy to pick a team," he says.

"I know my team. But the substitutes are the biggest problem.

"Some very good players are going to be left out. It is not easy to tell them that. The consolation for anyone who is not playing in the final is to be on the bench because they do then feel part of it.

"I hope that at some point in the Champions League they extend the substitutes bench to 11 outfield players as they do in World Cup games. I think that would be justified in the final.

"Quite simply the dilemma I have in deciding who is going to be on the bench and having to tell them that should be taken from me.

"It doesn't become easier for me. In fact it becomes more difficult because this team, for instance, are starting to blend together and mature together. You get to know them better.

"They know they have contributed a lot to the season. But to be left out and then to be told by me, it doesn't matter what I tell them, I don't think it registers or resonates with them at all. The disappointment is deep and it is understandable."

The Reds' young braves can write their own European chapter in Moscow.

With Munich survivors Sir Bobby Charlton, Harry Gregg, Bill Foulkes and Albert Scanlon watching in the Luzhniki Stadium, the burden of honouring the 50th anniversary of the 1958 air crash won't be far from the Reds thoughts.

There is also the blemish on Old Trafford's trophy-laden record that has witnessed only two European Cup final successes in 1968 and 1999 since the Babes first went into continental combat over five decades ago.

But manager Sir Alex Ferguson knows he has the players to rise to the challenge against Chelsea.

"I've said many times that our history is an illustrious history but there is a weakness in terms of the European trophies that we've won," he said in Russia.

"I hope we can go some way towards making that better tonight. We've had ten days' good preparation. It's been a long season with lots of stresses and pressures, but it's given the players an opportunity to do some serious work on the training field.

"We're in our best shape. It should give us a good opportunity to win this final.

"You're judged by what you win as a team. This team has an opportunity tonight to answer comparisons with 1999.

"If we win and achieve what they did in '99, we'll be very proud of them and we will have justified our opinion of them.

"It's a very good Manchester United team emerging, and we've got a very high opinion of them.

"It's important I trust my players. We may not have the overall experience of Chelsea given the players we have, but we have the nerve and the courage."

Cristiano Ronaldo and Wayne Rooney are the elite names of the Reds' burgeoning group of young talent.

But the United boss doesn't want the team to rely on just the two of them in Moscow.

"Many of my players are young. The likes of Cristiano Ronaldo and Wayne Rooney have big futures ahead of them," he added.

"In terms of their ability, temperament and courage to play, this is a big stage of course. But it's the same for all of our players. We can't rest on two young lads as our overall saviours tonight.

"I'll be depending on all 11 players. It's a massive challenge, but we can do it."

The stats and strength may not be on United's side in the Champions League Final but Sir Alex Ferguson still slept soundly in Moscow on the eve of the match.

Physically the Reds boss admits that Chelsea's brute force outpoints United's power.

He was also surprised to be informed in a pre-match press conference in Russia at the Luzhniki Stadium that his record against the Londoners has been just one win in the last 13 matches with the Euro final opponents gaining seven victories since 2003.

"We've been praised this season so we're doing something right," Sir Alex replied.

"Our record demands respect. What can I say? You mention my record. It's a bad one. I didn't know that, but I don't pay attention to the things I lose.

"However, tonight I think I've got the players to do the job and I trust that.

"Chelsea are a physically stronger team than most of the Premier League teams. They base a lot of their play on that strength.

"But we don't need to match that. We can concentrate on our movement and passing, our strengths. I think we're good at that.

"We do, though, have to pay attention to the strengths of Chelsea, of Drogba, Ballack and Lampard. Part of our preparation has been about that.

"Playing a team you know well means you probably add more detail for the preparation. We'll analyse Chelsea over the last year and the games against them, some of the more important games we've played against them.

"But generally that's normal for a final. A final requires complete appraisal of your opponents' strengths and weaknesses.

"But ultimately you have to trust your own players, and I do that absolutely."

One of those defeats against Chelsea came 12 months ago in the FA Cup Final when once again United entered a showpiece event against the Stamford Bridge side as newly crowned Premiership title winners.

Sadly at Wembley, the Reds were beaten 1-0 by an extra-time Didier Drogba winner.

"We're fresher than the Cup Final. We're much fitter after ten days' preparation, though that applies to Chelsea also," added the United manager.

"In last year's final we were at the point after playing so many games with the same 11 or 12 players that we had no real reserve to change a game in the final.

"This year we have. That will make a difference. Sometimes the game is won by your substitutions. We're in a stronger position now than we were last year.

"We'll have to play our best game. You don't have possession for 100% of the game, or absolute control for 100% of the game. Your opponents play a part.

"But we know the strengths and weaknesses of Chelsea so we go into the game on an equal footing."

United's 60 minutes training session on the Moscow pitch 24 hours before the final was followed by Chelsea's work out and appeared to allay fears about the state of the Luzhniki surface.

When England played their Euro 2008 qualifier here last year it was on an artificial surface but UEFA insisted grass was laid for the Champions League Final.

The Russian hosts complied in April but it has needed another relaying with imported grass from Slovakia at a cost of £160,000, overseen by English groundsman Matt Frost.

He was reported to have been disappointed with the new natural surface but Fergie was philosophical. He said, "I've no concerns about it. UEFA have done their best and the fact they've relayed it from Astroturf to turf is a big delight. Remember Old Trafford in January and February is not the best and probably the worst in the league, so there are no worries for me."

While Fergie is a veteran of three European finals having won the European Cup Winners' Cup with Aberdeen in 1983 and with United in 1991, plus the Champions League in 1999, by contrast, Chelsea boss Avram Grant is a big stage novice.

However, the Scot doesn't believe it gives him an advantage: "I don't think it helps. I remember going up against Alfredo Di Stefano (at Real Madrid) in my first final and I didn't shrivel.

"I handed him a bottle of whisky! It's an opportunity for Avram Grant. It's a chance for us both in a well balanced game."

Rio Ferdinand is hell bent on becoming a member of an elite group of Reds and being recognised as a true Manchester United player.

The select band are those United players who have a European Cup winners' medal in their collection.

Despite three Premiership title wins in 2003, 2007 and 2008, the 29-year-old doesn't expect to be enrolled in the Old Trafford Hall of Fame until he can boast the same achievement as the 1968 and 1999 Euro heroes.

"In my eyes anyway, to be considered a real Manchester

United player, you need to be part of a winning Champions League team," the England defender says.

"That is my view. This club has got great traditions, great history and a great winning mentality. They have won League championships and enjoyed great European nights. Those sides are revered and remembered by everyone.

"So to be part of a winning Champions League team would put us up there among those kind of guys. That is where you aim to be."

Medals around his neck are the only style accessories Ferdinand wants to wear these days.

Rightly or wrongly the Londoner has often been cited as your typical over-paid, partying superstar footballer who epitomises everything that is wrong in the 21st-century player.

But Ferdinand, who could lead the Reds out in Moscow tomorrow night if Ryan Giggs isn't chosen in Sir Alex Ferguson's starting XI, believes the image is now all wrong:

"When I left West Ham to join Leeds in 2001 it was a conscious decision to move out of London," he said.

"I could have stayed with clubs in London after I left Upton Park but I made a conscious decision to get out of London because I was enjoying the finer things in life rather than the football.

"Since I've been here I've been a good pro in terms of picking the right times to go out. I'm not going to lie, I'm no different, everyone likes a good night out at the right times. But you can't do it at the wrong times at Manchester United because you will get found out.

"When you come to Manchester United it does mature you. It is the workload you have, it is the fact that there are so many games that you cannot afford to go out, it is the profile you have.

"You have to learn very quickly how to conduct your life outside of football. Otherwise you will be quickly out of the door and people will have forgotten you ever came."

Having signed for the Reds from Leeds after World Cup 2002 for £30m, Ferdinand went through the torment of his missed drugs chapter and subsequent eight-month ban in 2004.

Many United fans turned on him when his contract saga blew up only 12 months later.

Despite eventually putting pen to paper on a new deal he had ground to make up in the popularity contests.

"I knew when I signed that contract in 2005 that I had to change the opinions people had of me," added Rio.

"The proof of the pudding's in the eating and I think I've done that.

"The worst time was being booed by my own supporters. Circumstances were not great at the time – there was the incident when me and my agent were in the same restaurant as Chelsea chief executive Peter Kenyon. In hindsight it could have been avoided but you live and learn.

"The manager just said to me that I had to keep playing my normal game. He said it would take time to get people back on side. But they will realise you want to be at the club when you go out there on the pitch.

"All I have ever tried to do is to be consistent over a long period of time. I was always associated with the bling culture but whoever knows me knows that for the best part of six years I haven't been into bling.

"OK, I like a nice watch, drive a nice car and wear nice clothes but being bling means spending money on willy-nilly things, having no respect for the game and it was the sort of thing I was accused of.

"To me, that is unwarranted. But people have assumptions about the way you are."

European Cup goal hero Ole Gunnar Solskjaer believes United can emulate the 1999 Champions League winners in Moscow – and then eclipse them by adding more Euro glory.

Sir Alex Ferguson has lamented that the Reds have not delivered enough European Cups for a club of Old Trafford's size and history.

After 1968, Matt Busby's Wembley heroes failed to add to their triumph.

The treble-winning boys of 1999 were expected to build on Solskjaer's winner in the 2-1 Nou Camp success against Bayern Munich. But less than two years later Bayern were beating United in the quarter-finals and captain Roy Keane famously declared in Germany that the historic side might need dismantling.

Solskjaer, however, suspects Fergie's latest crop will avoid suggestions of such drastic actions:

"Hopefully, next Wednesday will be the start of something more than we achieved," the Reds legend said.

"That team in 1999 achieved it once. It was a fantastic feeling. The memories of that night stick with you forever.

"I wanted to experience more of them and believed we could but we never got round to it. Nine years have gone by before the club could get back to a final.

"This side can win it and hopefully that will start something bigger. You want them to get the feeling that this is where we want to be every year.

"Hopefully, it will inspire them and motivate them to believe what they really can achieve because I believe this team and these players can achieve a lot more.

"I do think this team could go on to win more Champions Leagues than us because of the talent in the side and the age of the players.

"If you can give Cristiano Ronaldo and Wayne Rooney, for instance, the taste of what it is like to win the Champions League at this club, they will get the impetus to win it again and again.

"Cristiano's personality is such that he wants to improve and he wants to be the best; 41 goals is unbelievable from a player who has played mostly on the wing setting up other people and providing so much else on the pitch."

Wayne Rooney is geared up for payback time against Chelsea in Moscow.

The black days in Rooney's career story have involved the Londoners in some shape or form.

In his debut campaign for the Reds in 2005 he had to

applaud Chelsea onto Old Trafford in May as League Champions.

In 2006 the United striker broke his foot at Stamford Bridge, putting his England World Cup hopes in jeopardy.

He missed the start to the finals in Germany as a result and then in the quarter-finals against Portugal he tangled with Ricardo Carvalho and was sent off in Gelsenkirchen for stamping on the Chelsea defender.

This season he scored at Stamford Bridge but aggravated a hip injury in United's April defeat.

But now is time to even things up.

"I hope it is payback time. I have certainly had a few ups and downs against Chelsea," says the 22-year-old.

"There have been some bad memories but hopefully now this is going to be a good one.

"The World Cup was a big lesson. I have spoken to Carvalho a couple of times since and he is a nice guy. There is no problem with him. He is a good, honest player.

"In fact he is probably the hardest defender I have ever played against. He is strong and quick. He reads the game very well. They also have John Terry who is big and strong and never gives in. They complement each other well.

"Chelsea are a difficult team to play against. They are big and physical. They also have players who can win the game for them from nothing.

"We know it is going to be difficult. The games we have had with them this season have been fairly close so we are ready for a tough game.

"We have to go into the game and relax and play the football we know we can. If we go defensive then Chelsea are a good enough team to punish us. We have to relax and play the free flowing football we have done most of the season.

"We have to seize the moment. Opportunities like this don't come round all the time and we have to make the most of it.

"You can never take anything for granted. It might never happen again. It is very rare teams get to the Champions League Final almost every year."

Rooney has become a two-times Premier League champion with the Reds ever since his £30m move from Everton in 2004. Now he wants to showcase his ability on the biggest Euro stage.

"I have always said that personally I prefer to win the Premier League and I have done that again this year," he added.

"That is a great honour but it would be nice to win the Champions League. That would be unbelievable.

"It hurt me to see Liverpool do so well in it. It was painful when they won it. But this is a great opportunity for all our lads.

"You join Manchester United to win things. I have managed to do that and to now reach the Champions League Final is a great achievement by the team.

"I am sure a lot of the Everton fans may understand now. If they didn't understand before I hope they do now.

"You always get recognised as a better player by playing in the Champions League Final. You look at last year and I thought Cristiano Ronaldo deserved to be the World Player of the Year but Kaka got it.

"I think the main reason he did that was because he got to the final and won it with Milan. To play in the final is to show the world what you can do."

FINAL PREMIERSHIP TOP FOUR PRE CHELSEA MAY 21							
	P	W	D	L	F	A	PTS
UNITED	38	27	6	5	80	22	87
Chelsea	38	25	10	3	62	26	85
Arsenal	35	24	11	3	74	31	83
Liverpool	36	21	13	4	67	28	76

United are the Champions of England and Sir Alex Ferguson says the title winners are "bouncing" to Moscow.

After securing their place in the Champions League Final at the expense of Barcelona, the Reds beat West Ham 4-1 at Old Trafford.

Chelsea won at Newcastle 48 hours later to set up a final day title shoot-out with United away at Wigan and Avram Grant's side at home to Bolton.

Both title rivals' last day opponents had escaped relegation before the final 90 minutes of the League campaign.

Cristiano Ronaldo scored from the spot at Wigan in the first half to make it advantage United.

But then news came that Andre Shevchenko had scored against Bolton to set up a nail-biting finale.

The dramatic script saw Ryan Giggs come off the bench to equal Sir Bobby Charlton's 35-year record as Old Trafford's all-time appearance maker.

On his 758th appearance, Giggs scored at Wigan to effectively seal the title win with 90 minutes to go.

A late Bolton equaliser meant United had won the championship by two points to kick off wild celebrations at the JJB.

It was a poignant moment when Roger Byrne junior, son of United's 1958 captain who perished in the Munich air crash, brought the Premiership crown onto the pitch to be presented to United.

As he hailed the Reds' tenth Premiership title win, Sir Alex Ferguson warned beaten rivals Chelsea and European Cup final opponents the psychological advantage was with United.

"If we had lost the title it would have been a great knock but the great thing is we are bouncing into the final," he said.

He also turned his attentions to Liverpool's record of 18 top-flight titles as the Reds moved to within one of the Anfielders.

"I think it will come. This side is young. There is plenty left in them."

Ryan Giggs couldn't contain his delight having scored the goal that sealed his and United's tenth Premier League crown.

"It feels great," he said of his record-extending tenth title.

Giggs had played down the probable personal achievement of equalling Sir Bobby Charlton's record as the matches were ticked off to the 758 figure.

But, having levelled with the 1968 European Cup and 1966 World Cup winner, Giggs had to abandon his "personal records are to tell the grandchildren" stance.

"Yes, it's great. To equal someone like Sir Bobby, who was watching me play for Salford Boys when I was 13, 14 and then for the youth team," said Ryan.

"He is probably United's greatest ever player who stands for everything Manchester United stands for, so it is special.

"I won't try to play that down. It is special. Then to win the championship and to score a goal, well, it's great for me.

"But I'll enjoy the moment then get ready for next week. It's how it has to be. You can't look back. You have to look forward.

"Winning the league feels great, and hopefully we can win another trophy in Moscow."

Cristiano Ronaldo believes United were worthy winners of the Premier League title.

"The pressure was high, but we believed in ourselves and we deserved to win the title," he said.

Ronaldo's 31 league goals in 34 games played a major part in delivering United's capture of the crown, but he says praise cannot be heaped on one player:

"This was a team effort and I think we deserved it because we are the best team in the Premier League."

Michael Carrick headed to the Champions League Final believing that United have firmly proved they are the best team in the Premier League.

"At the start of the campaign we wanted to prove that the previous season's title was not a one-off, we really were the best team.

"But the season was not as straightforward as the previous one. We did not start in particularly great form, we were behind Arsenal and people were saying it was over.

"So to come out on top is very satisfying, we really earned it this time around. To win the league and be in the final of the Champions League, that is what this club is all about.

"The key to our success has been determination, and the discipline within the squad. The boss made some signings

last summer that really strengthened the squad as a whole and that has proved the case in recent months when everyone has played their part in a massive way.

"If it was not for the numbers and quality that we had in the squad, who knows, we might not be sitting in this position.

"We get on so well, even the lads that came during the summer and did not speak much English when they first arrived. But they were willing to try to interact with the lads and the British lads really appreciate that.

"We have a good laugh about it when they get things wrong but they are willing to try and learn. The performances on the pitch speak for themselves but as characters within the squad the team spirit has been fantastic."

Edwin Van der Sar can now truly celebrate United's club-record defensive display. Only seven goals conceded at Old Trafford in the Premier League and just 15 away from home adds up to a measly 22 in the 'goals against' column.

But placing the League medal around his neck meant the Dutch keeper could finally be satisfied with his defensive achievement.

"Defensive records are not a major thing unless you win something at the end of it all," Edwin said.

"When I was at Juventus we had the best defensive record in Serie A in the two years I was in Turin, but we didn't win the league in either campaign, so it didn't mean a thing.

"If we had lost the title on the last day to Chelsea then our great record wouldn't have added up to much either. It would have gone down in the record books but I couldn't have celebrated it.

"As a defence we have done well but that is because we have had others in the team working hard to help us.

"Likewise, the forwards score because the defence gives them a sound base. It is a team thing and it is a great team."

Van der Sar won his first English title 12 months ago when Chelsea drew at Arsenal while United weren't playing.

"It is so much better to actually win it on the day. This feels so much better than last year," he added.

"I was grateful to win it last year and I was very happy but this has felt so much better. It might mean having to go through a few anxieties, but it was all worth it."

colleagues promoting sportswear. It is accompanied by the slogan: Together, Impossible Is Nothing.

United would be a more appropriate vehicle for the advertisers.

In 1958, it seemed impossible that the Reds would return as a major force from the ruins of Munich.

In 1968, at half time in the Bernabeu and 3-1 down to Real Madrid in the European Cup semi-final, it seemed impossible United could ever deliver the poignant prize to Matt Busby.

In 1999, with 90 minutes on the Nou Camp clock and trailing Bayern Munich 1-0, it seemed impossible that

the Reds would commemorate what would have been Busby's 90th birthday and secure the Champions League trophy for Alex Ferguson.

In December 2005, returning form Portugal after losing to Benfica and being dumped out of the Champions League at the group stage with a transitional period underway and Roman Abramovich pumping untold roubles into Chelsea, it seemed impossible that the Reds would only be 18 months away from becoming England's major power again.

Impossible is not in the Old Trafford vocabulary.

It was a nerve-shattering way to settle the ultimate

club prize but the Reds stood firm and saved Cristiano Ronaldo what would have been the cruellest of endings to his fabulous season.

It had just turned 1.30 in the morning in Russia and the birds were just emerging from their slumber before dawn broke when 37-year-old veteran Edwin Van der Sar saved from Nicolas Anelka in a sensational do-or-die spot-kick finale.

It was hoped England's two most powerful outfits could produce a thriller worthy of the first all-English European Cup final. They didn't disappoint.

United had started with an experienced midfield with Paul Scholes getting his final chance as promised alongside Michael Carrick and 2001 Champions League winner Owen Hargreaves.

But the midfield and attacking combination, with Ronaldo, Rooney and Tevez added to the trio at the heart of the engine room, meant a six-strong unit that had never actually started a game together!

On paper, it had the same lopsided look the team-sheet had in 1999 when Ryan Giggs played on the right with licence to roam and Jesper Blomqvist occupied the left flank. This time it was Hargreaves wearing the latest of his many hats as a wide right-winger.

For 90 minutes that night in Spain was United's most ineffective Euro display of the campaign and there was some concern that a new-look midfield coupled with the three forwards may find themselves similarly befuddled by the system. But United fitted the system this time like a glove.

The pre-match on-field extravaganza that greeted the 22 players was pure theatre and drama. It certainly asked a lot of the players to live up to when the balloons and red-and-gold cloaked dancers departed to leave the stage for the Reds and Blues.

For 15 minutes it was no contest. Bring back the balloons!

It looked likely the two combatants were dug in for a possible repeat of the FA Cup Final bore last May, but then the safety trigger came off and the dancing girls were forgotten.

A step-over piece of Ronaldo magic broke the spell of doom when he outwitted Essien with a wave of the leg. It was to be a significant individual duel.

Inevitably, there was a sprinkling of irritation on the cards and the first flashpoint arrived in the 21st minute. Scholes and Makelele smashed into each other in an aerial clash. Chelsea got the free kick, Essien got a yellow card and Scholes got a booking and a bloody nose. He ended up looking like Ricky Hatton after his Las Vegas brawl with Floyd Mayweather.

Scholes returned from treatment to help carve out United's opener.

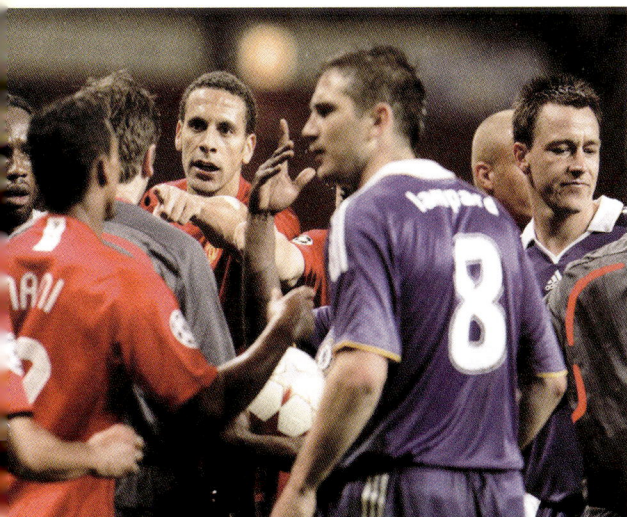

United were on the march and Chelsea had little answer to the rampant Reds. It should have been 2-0 after 35 minutes and would have been but for the sensational double intervention of keeper Petr Cech.

He saved Tevez's close-range diving header and then steadied himself to put a stiff right arm in the way of Carrick's measured follow up.

While the Reds have been driven by their historical destiny this season, England midfielder Lampard has been on his own fate crusade following the death of his mother only weeks before the final

Whoever up there was guiding this final, it wasn't going to be one-sided and when Essien's shot was deflected by Nemanja Vidic and then Rio Ferdinand, it wrong-footed Edwin Van der Sar and Lampard was powering in from deep to slide in the equaliser.

For the Reds it was a goal out of the Busby Babes' handbook.

Local products Scholes and Wes Brown engineered it with a brilliant one-two to flummox Frank Lampard on the right wing. Mancunian Brown's cross was met with a leap and power header from Ronaldo that those with longer memories will tell you was out of Munich victim Tommy Taylor's repertoire.

The all-English final was living up to the hype of its bread and butter product, the Premier League. But then the Champions suddenly went AWOL as a force and the powerful Londoners took a firm grip on the showpiece.

It was ugly in parts, as you'd expect from Chelsea, but United had little answer as the midfield became overrun.

The Reds were under the cosh as Essien thumped one over, Vidic was forced to dive to clear for a corner and

then Ballack arrived onto the ball. An ex-Munich player scoring in the 58th minute? Surely not. Fate couldn't be that cruel.

The Reds survived that moment and then escaped an even bigger let-off when Drogba smacked a post in the 78th minute.

But this was how it was in '99, with Bayern striking woodwork as United struggled to produce their swagger of earlier rounds.

Where was the Teddy Sheringham or the Ole Gunnar Solskjaer? Had United got a hero?

When Ryan Giggs came on to become the club's all-time No. 1 appearance-maker with three minutes to go, the stage was set for a fairytale ending.

Chelsea, though, looked like they may have spent all their energy in 90 minutes. As physios, medics and management came onto the pitch for the pre-extra time administration of orders and muscle rubs, a handful of Avram Grant's side lay on the turf receiving treatment while all the Reds stayed on their feet.

The Giggs fairytale storyline was a whisker away from fruition in extra time when he stabbed a golden opportunity after Evra's superb penetrating run. But somehow Terry got his head on the goal-bound effort to deflect it away.

Just like the Premier League title race, this was going to go down to virtually the last kick – or last slap, in Drogba's case. The Ivory Coast striker tarnished England's big night with a 116th-minute red card for striking Nemanja Vidic.

His exit was to prove significant as the rain poured and tired bodies were put through the nerve-shattering penalty shoot-out.

If you thought the 120 minutes of action had squeezed every last ounce of drama from this memorable encounter, then think again.

Potential heroes and potential villains stepped up to the plate as fans watched through outstretched fingers.

First to suffer the stomach-churning feeling of a miss was Ronaldo. This was one ending too vindictive to contemplate.

Then John Terry slipped and slammed his penalty against the post and United fans could look again.

The youngsters like Tevez, Nani and Anderson had done their bit in the 12-yard shoot-out. Now it was down to the veterans.

Giggs hit the sixth successful United kick out of seven and then Van der Sar took off to deny ex-Manchester City striker Nicolas Anelka and the United celebrations began.

UNITED:
Van der Sar; Brown (Anderson 120), Ferdinand, Vidic, Evra, Carrick, Hargreaves, Scholes (Giggs 87), Ronaldo, Rooney (Nani 101), Tevez.
Subs not used: Kuszczak, O'Shea, Fletcher, Silvestre.

CHELSEA:
Cech; Essien, Terry, Carvalho, A. Cole; Makelele (Belletti 120), Ballack, Lampard, Malouda (Kalou 92), J. Cole (Anelka 99), Drogba.
Subs not used: Cudicini, Shevchenko, Mikel, Alex.

Sir Alex Ferguson has vowed to be back in next year's Champions League Final.

"When you win something you have to look at the players' eyes to see if the hunger is there," he said after the Moscow triumph.

"Defending the European Cup is not an easy thing to do. I think the team is good enough and they will improve next year.

"The drama of the final does drain you. It is worth it, though, because to get success you have to get through the pain in a game like that and it is part of being the manager of this club.

"I'm proud of winning it because, as I've said many times, we should have won it more times. We have made one step forward towards getting a respectable figure in

> *"In 1999 I was 26. It was a blur and I will try to enjoy this a little bit more because there won't be too many more of these for me"*
> *– Ryan Giggs*

> **"Sometimes you have to pinch yourself but I don't get carried away, euphoria evaporates immediately. But that penalty save from Edwin Van der Sar was my moment, the emotion and the excitement and then you just carry on."**
> **– Sir Alex Ferguson**

terms of Champions League wins and we want to add more and get up there alongside the Liverpools, Bayern Munichs and Ajaxs.

"And then you never know what ambition can do to you. Real Madrid have nine wins and it is a target you

take for granted – perhaps not in my lifetime, but it is worth chasing.

"We have gone a long way to eradicating our record in the European Cup."

Ryan Giggs is the only United player to have appeared in two European Cup winning teams for the Reds.

Giggs is Old Trafford's appearance record holder now, with 759 games behind him and has won ten Premiership titles – but he wants more!

And the Welshman doesn't see a future away from Old Trafford.

"So it's great for us to be able to win the European Cup, particularly this year with it being the 50th anniversary of Munich.

"Fate does seem to have played a big part this season. Giggsy broke Bobby's record in Moscow, and what a night to do that. And it's 50 years since Munich, so maybe it was written in the stars.

"But you can't take that for granted. You don't take that as a given. We knew we'd have to work hard to become European champions and be standing where we are now."

"I feel very proud for the lads. They believe all the time. The lads deserve the Champions League. I looked forward to winning this competition — and we won the Premier League. It's a magnificent season for me. I thought, we're going to lose. I score the goal and then miss the penalty. The worst day of my life.

"But the lads did the job and I feel very proud for them. It means everything for me."

— Cristiano Ronaldo

"The most poignant thing for me was Bobby coming up to me and saying 'well done, you deserved it'. You could see he was really pleased for the lads.

"Manchester United runs through his veins and he's a legend, an inspiration to all of us players.

"It has been a long time since I felt like this — it's a huge emotion in my heart. When I was a child, I never thought I would be lifting the Cup, but dreams usually come true and I am very, very happy."

— Carlos Tevez

THE FANS' STORY

Celebrations surrounding Manchester United's success in reaching the European Champions League Final have been on hold for many fans as they struggle to make any sense of the visa requirements for entering Russia. With no announcements from Russian authorities, fans of both Manchester United and Chelsea have been left to wonder how or when they might complete the necessary paperwork to travel to Moscow for the final on May 21, or indeed whether any paperwork will be required.

This debacle will be frustrating for any fan attempting to forward plan their trip. It is anticipated that more than 40,000 Chelsea and United fans will travel to Moscow for the game.

To leave fans in the dark for so long is unfair and insulting and we trust that the Russian authorities will make up for their shortcomings by serving as the best possible hosts on the day.

"Our name was on the trophy. I felt a bit sorry for John Terry when he slipped — but his misfortune is our good luck. It's a magic feeling."

Kenny Pritchard, Cheadle Hulme

United fans on a budget are going the distance for Champions League glory in Moscow. Instead of booking direct charter or scheduled flights, they are going the long way round. Taking advantage of cut-price airlines and an epic 17-hour train ride, they hope to arrive in time for kick-off on Wednesday, May 21. In total, the trip-on-a-budget will cost just £205.

One of the fans is life-long Red Damien O'Sullivan. His trip will start at Birmingham Airport with a flight to Dublin with Ryanair on the Monday morning. After a pint or two of Guinness and a three-hour wait, he and his three mates board a plane for Riga, capital of Latvia, arriving at 7.50pm that night. The four stay overnight in Riga – no accommodation booked yet – and are due to board a train for Moscow at 4.15pm local time on the Tuesday. They have booked a cabin with bunk beds for the journey of 17 hours and 26 minutes.

They arrive in Moscow at 9.50am on the day of the match. The next day, they head back to Riga by train, arriving at 10.20am local time on the Friday. Their Ryanair flight to Bristol leaves at 10.55pm and arrives 11.55pm. With the money they have saved, Damien, his pals Damian Donnelly, Ian Weston and Paul Manning, plan on lording it for the last leg of their trip – a taxi from the airport back to their homes in Birmingham. Each of them has paid £105 for their return flights and another £100 for their train journeys. Their route covers 4,144 miles – 909 miles more than simply flying to Moscow and back – but is a lot cheaper.

Damien, 27 an IT worker who used to live in Wilmslow, said: "It's a long way round but it is much cheaper and it should be a good laugh."

United fan Martin Sheehan is taking the slow route to Moscow for the Champions League Final – for £85 return. The 25-year-old call centre worker set off yesterday on his trek, which will take four flights and two bus rides to get to and from the Wednesday final. He is one of a band of travel-wise Reds saving a fortune by avoiding more direct routes to Moscow, with some flights costing more than £1,000.

The six-day return journey started when Martin, from Old Trafford, and four pals boarded a flight from Liverpool to Stockholm. They stayed there overnight before boarding a flight today for Riga, in Latvia, where they get on a bus tomorrow for a 14-hour drive to Moscow. With no room booked in Moscow – the city is sold out – Martin hopes to celebrate a United win through the night before getting on a bus back to Riga, followed by return flights to Stockholm and then Liverpool – landing at 8pm on Friday.

"It was the same in Barcelona in 1999 and in 1968 at Wembley. I don't think United were the best team on either of those occasions. And I have to say that United were very lucky here again."

Alan Shrager, Whitefield

MAY 19

Manchester's exodus to Moscow began in earnest today. Thousands of United fans started the long journey to Red Square ahead of Wednesday's Champions League Final against Chelsea. The two clubs have each sold 21,000 tickets for the match. Two direct flights were leaving for Moscow this morning but United supporters were also boarding planes for Prague, Stuttgart and Paris. Fans at Manchester Airport spoke of their hopes for the game despite spending a fortune getting to Russia.

But as fans left for Moscow, those staying behind have reacted with fury as plans for a United victory parade remained in the balance. Just two days before the final, it is still not clear if Reds fans will be allowed to cheer their heroes on the city streets later this week. Supporters groups have called on council chiefs, police and the club to hammer out an agreement in time for the big match. Sean Bones, of fans' group Shareholders United, said fans were furious there might not be a parade. He said: "We have won the Premier League and the fans should be able to thank the players and the manager."

Devastated Manchester United fan Neil Stock was refused entry into Russia because a page was missing from his passport. The sandwich shop owner from Stockport landed at Moscow's Domodedovo Airport, where he was told by immigration officials he would not be admitted into the country. Despite frantic appeals to the immigration offices and also a call to the British Embassy, Neil was forced to fly back home.

He paid £500 for a flight back to Gatwick Airport from where he took another jet for £300 to Manchester Airport. He had already paid £2,500 for his original flight and accommodation for three nights in Moscow, as well as a ticket for the final. He arrived back at his home in Heaviley just after 9pm last night.

Neil said: "I'm absolutely devastated. I think it will sink in a bit later when I realise I won't be watching the game there. What they did was bang out of order. My passport is nine years old and the page must have just fallen out. I don't know how it happened. I didn't even know it was missing. Of course I protested but they didn't listen. In fact they were laughing because I was saying I had paid £2,500 for the trip. It's very cruel."

"I have never gone through so much emotion at a football match in my entire life."

Dave Hart, Swindon

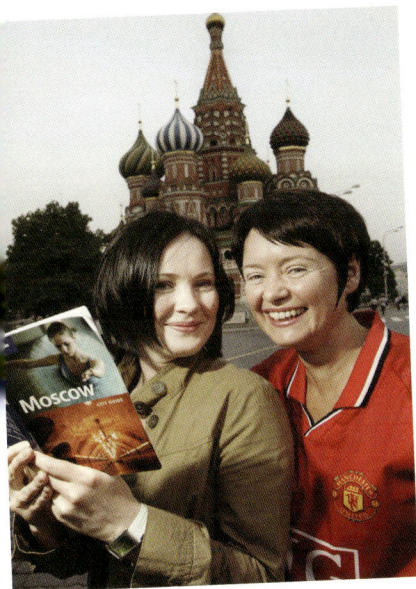

An international mercy mission today reunited a desperate Reds fan with his missing ticket for tonight's Champions League Final. Archie Moore, 50, from Stockport, lost the golden ticket as he dashed through security at Manchester Airport at the last minute before flying to Moscow, via Frankfurt. Security staff picked it up and tried frantically to find him before he boarded his plane. They made repeated announcements in the departure lounge, but Archie only discovered he had lost his ticket when he arrived at Frankfurt – and officials would not let him fly on to the Russian capital without it. But the day was saved thanks to a police officer based at Manchester Airport.

PC Robin Murray, who has not missed a match at Old Trafford since 1990, traced Archie – then an operation swung into action to fly the ticket to Frankfurt in time, with a Lufthansa captain carrying Archie's ticket in his pocket as he flew from Manchester to Frankfurt at 7am today. The airline's ground crews raced to the plane after it touched down and then dashed to the terminal to put the ticket safely in Archie's hands. The overjoyed United fan then flew to the Russian capital on a re-booked Lufthansa flight at 1pm, just in time to get there for the match. He said: "I'm absolutely delighted that I've got my ticket. I can't thank everyone enough.

MAY 21

Today, as thousands of fans streamed into Moscow, police said there were no signs of any trouble. Chief Superintendent Janette McCormick, who is in Moscow with a team of police spotters, said: "There are no issues at the moment. We have no reports of any incidents."

"This is all the more special because it is the anniversary of the Munich air disaster. They have won it three times now and although we didn't play all that well, I think we played the game the way it should be played."

Stuart Andrew, Sale

MAY 21

It wasn't looking like a happy ending for five dedicated United fans trying to make their way to the final in a camper van. They were stopped at the Russian border – because they didn't have the logbook for their hired vehicle.

The group from Irlam had planned to travel 6,000 miles across Europe and back on an 11-day round trip to watch United. Now they face forking out £280 each for a flight from Riga in Latvia to Moscow. Martin Green, 31, said: "We're gutted. We've got full insurance for the van, as well as visas, passports, everything, but the border guards don't speak our language and we've just hit a brick wall."

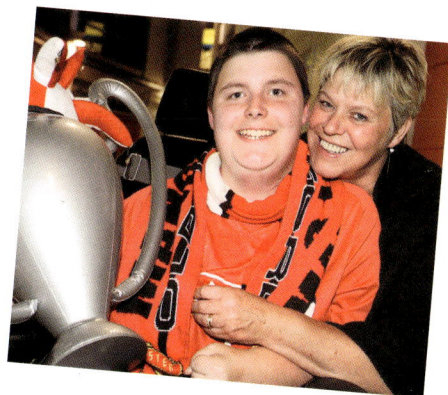

REECE ABBOTT
MARK ADAMS
ADNAN
STUART ADNETT
PETER WILLIAM ALKER
JIM ALLAN
ALBERT W. ALLEN
LUKE ALLEN
SHAUNA ALLEN
JAMES ALLINGTON
SIMON ANDERTON
MR ALAN ANDREW
PHILIP JOHN ANDREW
ALAN ANKERS
RYAN ANNETS
GEORGIA ANWAS
BEN APPLETON
EDWARD ARMITAGE
IAN ARMITAGE
DAVID ASHLEY
DAVID ASTON
JOHN ASHTON
JAMES ATKINSON
LIAM ATKINSON
JACK JOSEPH AXON-LOGAN
MIKE AYRES
BEN AZFAR
DAVID THOMAS BADROCK
MR STEPHEN BAILEY
STEVEN BAILEY
DOMINIC BAINES
SEAN DAVID BAINES
THOMAS BAINES
JAKE BAKER
JENNY BAKER
BALDEEP
STEVE BALDOCK
IAN BALDWIN
OLIVER BALL
MICHAEL BAMFORD
DARREN BANKS
JOSHUA JAMES BANKS
JENNIE BANNISTER
ALAN BARBER
JAMES BARKER
PAUL BARNETT
PATRICK BARRY
JASON BARTHOLOMEW
BRIAN GARETH BATES
BRIAN JOSEPH BATES
ELSIE BAXTER
STEVEN BAYLIS
GEORGE W. BEADSWORTH

LEE BEASLEY
KIERAN BEATTIE
PAUL BEAVER
ARTHUR BECKETT
CHRIS BEECH
DEREK J. BEECH
GEORGE BEECH
STEVE BEECH
MARTIN BEECHER
PAUL BELLWOOD
ADRIAN BENNETT
BRIAN BENNETT
GILLIAN BENNETT
JOSH BENSON
JAKE BENYON
ERNIE BERNARDY
SIMON BERNSTEIN
JOHN BERRY
SIMON BETHELL
STUART BICKERSTAFF
JOAN BILLINGHAM
BERNARD BILLINGTON
GARY BIRCHALL
DONALD BIRD
THOMAS BIRTWHISTLE
TREV (TISH) BISHOP
ROB BLADON
STUART BLAIKIE
BRADLEY JOHN BLEWITT
SAM BLINKHORN
DR. CRAIG PETER BLOMELEY
MR PETER PAUL BLOMELEY
MR ERIC BLOOD
JUSTIN MILBURN BLUNDELL
JACK BOARDMAN
TIAGO BOICA
LEE BOLAS
JOHN PATRICK BOLTON
CHRISTOPHER BOOTH
MARGARET BOOTH
MYLES BOOTH
NIGEL C. BOOTH
CHANTELLE BORROWDALE
DON BORTHWICK
DENNIS BOSTROM
JOE THE BIZZLE BOSWORTH
GEOFF BOUGHEY
MICHAEL BOULD
MARTIN BOWDEN
MR JOSEPH BOWERS
CHARLIE BOWLING
SEAN BOYLE
CHRISTOPHER BRACEWELL

DAVE BRADBURY
IAN BIG YAN BRADLEY
ROCKY BRADLEY
BILL & BILLY BRADSHAW JNR.
NATHAN & JOANNE
BRADSHAW
KARL BRAIDWOOD
SEAN LIAM BRANNIGAN
THOMAS BREHM
ALAN BRENNAN
PAUL BRENNAN
WINKIE BRENNAN
ANDREW BRERETON
GEORGE BRETTELL
CHRIS BREWARD
KEITH BRIDE
ZACK BRIERLEY
JAMES & STEVEN BRINDLEY
PIPPY BRISCOW
TIM BROADHURST
CHRIS, LEWIS & BOB BROOM
P. J. BROPHY
CATHERINE BROWN
JAMES CHRISTOPHER BROWN
NIALL BROWN
RAYMOND BROWN
LEE BROWNBILL
ANDREW BRUCE
CHRIS BRUCE
CRAIG BUCKLEY
SARAH BUCKLEY
THOMAS BUCKLEY
TREVOR BUCKLEY
STEVE BUNNEY
JIM BURBURY
PAUL BURGIN
NIGEL BURIN
STAN BURKE
WILLIAM BURKE
DAVID BURNS
DAVE BURROUGHS
ANTHONY (TONY) BURTON
JOLYON ISAAC BURTON
PETE BURTON
RYAN BUTCHER
GEOFF BUTT
CAMERON BUTTERWORTH
STUART BUTTON
BETHANY BYRNE
COLM BYRNE
CONNOR BYRNE
NICK CADMAN
LEE A. CALDEN

HAROLD CAMMISH
TREVOR HUGH CAMPBELL
MARK CARRIBAN
JAMES ANTHONY CARTY
CALLUM THOMAS CASE
ELLIOT CASS
STEPHEN ALUN CATTON
CHRISTINE CAUDWELL
CORDELIA CAVILL
OSCAR CAVILL
HING-POON CHAN
KATHERINE CHAN
DAVID CHAPMAN
GRAHAM CHAPMAN
LIAM ANTHONY CHAPMAN
GEORGINA CHAPPELL
CHARLES
RAYMOND CHARLES
ROY CHARLOTTE
JAMES CHARLSON
PAUL CHATTON
ADAM J. CHEESEMAN
WILLIAM CHEETHAM
CHLOE
FAHIM CHOWDHURY
CHRISTOPHER
DANIEL CLARE
RICK CLARE
ADAM CLARKE
SARAH CLARK
BILLY & LIAM CLARKE
JAMES A. CLARKE
ADAM CLAYTON
MANDY CLAYTON
HARRY DICK-CLELAND
VICKI DICK-CLELAND
RAYMOND CLOHERTY
JACK CLOSE
THOMAS CLYDE
ANDREW COATES
PAUL COATES
ROBERT COATES
NATHAN LEIGH COGBILL
BEN COGGIN
JON COLES
JAKE COLLEY
MATTHEW COLLINGE
SAM COLLINS
DAVID COLWELL
MARTIN THOMAS COMERFORD
PETER CONDE
DARREN CONNELL
STEPHEN CONNOLLY

RYAN GEORGE CONNOR
WILL CONNOR
CHRIS CONVILLE
CHARLES COOK
ROB COOK
MATTHEW COOKE
DEAN PAUL COOKSON
ALAN COOMBS
GARY COOMBS
MARK COOMBS
STEPHEN COOMBS
DENISE COOPER
JACK COOPER
PAUL COOPER
IAN COPELAND
ERIC CORBY
CONOR COSTELLO
TIM COSTELLO
PETER COTTRELL
MICHAEL COUGHLAN
LEE COULSON (COULEY)
LISA COULSON
CLAIRE COUZENS
MICK COUZENS
GLYN COWELL
LUKE STEVEN COYLE-MARSH
AMI COX
MR M. COX
CRAIG
CRANKIE
BEN CRAWFORD
MATTHEW CREELY
DANIEL CROMPTON
MATTHEW CROMPTON
STEVEN CROOK
ROBERT CROPPER
DANIEL CROSSFIELD
BEN CROWLEY
CLIVE ROBERT CRUMPTON
BRIAN CURLEY
ANTHONY CURRAN
MATTHEW CURRAN
ROWAN CURRAN
ALEXANDER CURTIS
FIONA CURTIS
TINA CURTIS
KIERAN J. DAINTREE
BETHANY DAKIN
ANDREW DALE
JODY DALY
JOHN DANIELS
KEN DANIELS
TERRY DANIELS

KEVIN DAUGHTRY
BRIAN DAVENPORT
PHIL DAVIDSON
ADAM DAVIES
BRIAN DAVIES
JAKE DAVIES
JANE DAVIES
JOHN DAVIES
JAMES DAVIS
PETER DAVIS
THOMAS DAVIS
ETHAN DAWSON
JANET DAY
DEBI, DANIELLE & LAUREN
DECLAN
RICHARD DENNETT
SARAH DERBYSHIRE
CAMERON LEIGH DEVANEY
ANDREW DICKERSON
LEONARD DIMMOCK
ADRIAN DINSMORE
EMMET DIVER
MARK & AARON DIXON
TYLER DOADES
MIKE DOBBIN
ANDREW DOBNEY
PETER DOCKRILL
JAMES DODD
MICHAEL DODD
RAYMOND DODD
PHIL DOHERTY
STEVE DONOGHUE (51)
STRETFORD ENDER SALFORD
JOE & LEAH DOOGAN
CHRIS DOONA
NATHAN DORAN
ETHAN DOUGAN
DREW ETHAN & JACEY
HOWARD DRONSFIELD
EDWARD DRZYMALA
MATTHEW DRZYMALA
STEVEN DUBBERLEY
SIMON PATRICK DUFF
GED DUFFY
JACK DUFFY
CHARLOTTE DUNCKER
BARRY DUNKERLEY
MIKE (DOGS) DONOHOE
MARC DUNSTAN
SAUL DYSON
JAKE EASTHAM
SUSAN EASTON
GLYN ANDREW EDWARDS

JULIE EDWARDS
MIKE EDWARDS
NEIL CHOC TAYLOR EDWARDS
PHILLIP EDWARDS
STUART EDWARDS
ANDREW ELLIOT
SELWYN ELLIOTT
BRIAN ELLIS
JAMES ENGLISH
ELIZABETH EVANS
MAX EVANS
MICHAEL EVANS
TREFOR EVANS
ALEX FAHY
CHRISTOPHER FAHY
PATRICK FAHY
JOHN FAIRLAMB
BRENT FAIRWEATHER
GEOFF FARRELL
CALLUM FARRER
LEWIS FARROW
TERRY FAWCETT
NEVILLE FEARICK
RICHARD FEEK
JAKE & TREV FELLOWS
PAUL FENNELL
SIMON FENNER
DION FENTON
JAKE FERGUSON
ELLIOT FIELDING
BENJAMIN FINE
BRETT FINE
AMY FAYE FINNEGAN
FR. BILL FINNEGAN
JOHN FINNEGAN
THOMAS FISH
BEN FLETCHER
JORDAN FLETCHER
LUKE FLETCHER
CHRISTOPHER FLOCKTON
DAVID FLOYD
PAUL FLYNN
MARTIN FOLEY
MARK ERIC FORD
JORDAN FORTUNE
ALLAN FOURACRE
JONATHAN FOWLER
DAVID FRANCIS
JAMIE FRANCIS
CLARE FRANKS
HECTOR FRASER
GILL FRICKER
LEE FRIEL

DAVID FRIEND
JAMES FROGGETT
ALEXANDER FRY
TIM FULLER
JOHN GALLAGHER
DAVID GALLIGAN
LUKA GALLIVER
JENNIE ISOBEL GAMMON
MR JOE GARNER
NICOLA GEDDES
PERIKLIS GEORGIADIS
MALCOLM GIBBONS
PAUL GIBSON
ALVIN GILLETT
CHARLES GILLHAM
ANTHONY GILLIGAN
JAKE GILLSON
MARCUS GILMORE
GRAHAM GLADWIN
MAURICE GLADWIN
BORIS GLAVAS
PETER GLEAVE
RICHARD GLEMMIE
GEORGE GLEN
LAWRENCE GLYNN
PERCY GOLDSMITH
DOMINIC GOOD
JACOB GOODMAN
CRÓNAN GOODMAN
DANIEL GORDON
GARY GORDON
SAMANTHA GORDON
MICK GORMAN
TOMMY GORMAN
CHRIS GORTON
DARREN GOULDEN
HENRY GOWDY
ANDREW R. GRAHAM
PETER GRAHAM
BRIAN GRANT
JOHN GRANT
BEN GRAY
DAVID GRAY
JOE GREEN
JEFF GREEN
NICK GREEN
DAVID GREENBANK
MIKKI GREENBANK
STEVE GREENHILL
LUKE GREENWOOD
AMANDA JAYNE GREGORY
BILLY GRIFFIN
BOBBY GRIFFIN

JAMES GRIFFITHS
PHIL GRIGG
ANTHONY GROSVENOR
TOM GRUNDON
E. GUNN
GURDEV
HAPPY 9TH BIRTHDAY CHRIS
HAIGH
AARON HAIRE
GEOFF HALFORD
MARY HALVEY
MATT HAMES
DAVE HAMILTON & BRETT
HAMILTON
KIEREN HAMILTON
GILES HAMPSON
ANTHONY HAND
OLIVER FOULKES HANNAM
KEITH & ANNE HANSON
STEVEN HARDICRE
MICK HARDMAN
JOHNATHAN MARK HARDY
PETER HARGREAVES
DANIEL HARPER
KEVIN MARTIN HARRIS
SUE HARRIS
CHRISTINE HARRISON
TERRY HARRISON
CARL, HARRY & EVIE FLETCHER
DAN HART
GEOFFREY HART
KEVIN HART
TREVOR HARVEY
JOHN HASLAM
MATHEW HASLAM
IAN HAWKSEY
TONY HAYDEN
ALEXANDER HAYES
PETER HAYES
MICHAEL HAYNES
SAM HAYWARD
RICHARD HEAD
ANN HEALEY
MICK HEARTFIELD
CASPER HEISELBERG
MARC & DEBORAH HENRY
JOSHUA HERBERT
GEOFFREY HERRING
JOHN HEYES
PAUL HIBBERT
BRIAN HICKLING
CHRISTOPHER HIGGINS
KAREN HIGGINS

NORMAN HILL	JAMIE	JACK YAN KORNY
STEPHEN HILL	JAKE JAMIESON	STEVEN YAN KORNY
ADAM HIRD	JULIE JARVIS	GARRY KYNASTON
SAM HIRST	ANDY JEEVES	SYRIL JOHN LACEY
SIMON HIRST	MATTHEW JENKINS	JONATHAN LAMB
PHILIP HODSON	ROBERT JENKINS	DAVE LAMBERT
DANIEL HOGAN	PETER JENKINSON	LEE LANCASTER
PHILIP HOLDING	MRS PAT JENNER	LISABETH LANCASTER
RICHARD HOLLAND	JOHN	GARETH LANG
GLENN HOLLAND	RAYMOND JOHN	MIKE LANGFORD
JOANNE HOLLIDAY	CRAIG JOHNS	MICHAEL LATIMER
VIC HOLLINGSWORTH	ROBERT H. JOHNS MBE	JAMES LAWRIE
JASON HOLMES	PETER JOHNSON	JOHN LAWSON
MICHAEL HOLMES	SEAN & TOM JOHNSTON	DAVID LAWTON
STEPHEN HOLMES	LIAM JOLLEY	DAVE LEADLEY
WAYNE, JAMIE & TERRI HOLT	JONATHAN & LYNNE	MRS BERYL LEARY
BEN HOLTBY	BRIAN JONES	STEVEN LEECH
KEITH HOOK	DREW BRANDON JONES	MAZ BEECH & STE LEES
PAUL HOOPER	GEORGE KIRBY JONES	ANDREW LEIGH NZ
SAHAL HOOSEN	GREG JONES	BRENT LEVER
MARTIN HOPE	IAN JONES	KELLY LEWIS
ROBERT HOPE	JOHN JONES	JOHN RICHARD LEWIS
JACK HORNBY	KEITH JONES	SZU-YI LIAO
GRAHAM HORSFAL	LEON CRAIG JONES	DESMOND LIBURD
GRAHAM STEWART HORTH	PAWEL FRYZJER KAKOWSKI	DAVID LIGHTFOOT
DESMOND HOUGH	MATTHEW KAYE	RALPH LILLYMAN
PHILLIP ROLF HOUGH	LEE ALAN KEARNEY	BRIAN ALAN LINDSAY
THOMAS EDWARD HOUGH	EAMON KEEGAN (LURGAN)	JIM LITTLEPROUD
JULIE HOUGHTON	MALACHY KEEGAN (LURGAN)	MICHAEL LIVINGSTONE
ALLEN HOWARD	TONY KEEGAN (LORD RAGLAN)	ALAN LLOYD
NICOLA HUDSON	GEOFFREY KEEN	KEVIN LLOYD
RYAN HUDSON	GEORGE EDWARD KEITHLEY	MALCOLM LLOYD
WESLEY HUDSON	KELLY	GLEN OWEN LOCKIE
CIARAN JOHN HUGHES	BOB KELLY	EMMA LOCKLIN
DAVID HUGHES	JOHN KELLY	MICHAEL LOFTUS
MICHAEL HUGHES	SEAN KELLY	TREVOR LOGAN
WILLIAM HUGHES	LYONS KENDALL	IAN LOMAS
DAVID HUNT	PAUL KERFOOT	ANDREW LONGWORTH
JOSHUA THOMAS HUNT	DAVID KERSHAW	GARETH LORD
JOHN HUNTER	OMAR KHOKHAR	GRAHAM LORD
ANDREW HUSH	MIKE KIBBLE	JOHN LORD
MR BRIAN HUTTON	TOMMY KIERMAN	REG LORD
JAMES HYDE	SEBASTIAN KILBURN	SAM LORD
JOHN HYNARD	JASON KILROY	JOYCE LORKING
JOSHUA HYNARD	GERALD KIMMINS	ANDY LOWE
ISAAC	ANDREW KINDER	DEAN RICHARD LOWE
CHRISTOPHER G. JACKSON	DAVID KING	LYNNE SUSAN LUCAS
CONNOR JACKSON	MICHAEL KING	MILES LUTKIN
DUNCAN JACKSON	NEIL KING	ADAM J. LYNCH
NEIL JACKSON	ANDY KIRK	PHILIP LYNCH
PAUL JAGGARD	SUE KIRKBY	ROBERT & MARK LYNCH
NEIL JAKUBIAK	ANDREW KNOWLES	ROD LYTLE
DAVID JAMESON	C. KNOWLES	DREW MACLEOD

TONY MADDEN
KATE MAGGS & JOHN GURD
GARY MAGUIRE
MAKI
GIOVANNI ANTONIO
MALACRINO
MANCHESTER KEV
MANCHESTER UNITED
SUPPORTERS CLUB
(BIRMINGHAM BRANCH)
DAVID MANNION
FRANK MANNION
IAN T. MARCHMENT
MARK
STEWART MARKEY
DAVID MARSHALL
GARY MARSHALL
MR PETER MARSHALL
PHIL MARSHALL
DEAN MARSLAND
ANTHONY H. MARTIN
CHRISTOPHER F. MARTIN
MARK MARTIN
MICHAEL F. MARTIN
TONY MARTIN
JON MASHHADI
LEWIS MASON
RICHARD MASON
PETER MASSEY
KAYLUM MATTHEWS
RICHARD MAXIM
THOMAS MAYBURY
DARREN MAYHEW
STEVEN MAYO
TANAYA MAYOH
ANTHONY MCCARRON
ALEC MCALPINE
JAMIE MCALPINE
TALC MCALPINE
PHILIP MCBRIDE
LOUIS & LUCAS MCCARTHY
JOHN MCCULLOUGH
PATRICK MCFADDEN
TOM MCFARLANE
JAMES MCGANN
ANTHONY MCHALE
SIMON MCILVANNEY
GEORGE MCINTYRE
PETER MCINTYRE
LAURA MCKANE
PATRICK MCKEOWN
PAUL MCKINLEY
DENIS MCLAUGHLIN

PATRICK MCLAUGHLIN
HARRY MCLEAN
SIMON MCLEAN
JAMES MCNAIR
DAMIAN MCNAMEE
TERRENCE E. MCNAMEE
ADAM MCWILLIAMS
ANTHONY MCWILLIAMS
NEIL G. MEEHAN
PAUL METCALFE
ADAM PHILIP MIDDLETON
PHILIP I. MIDDLETON
MATTHEW MIFSUD
STEVEN MILES
ANDREW MILLAR
DAN MILLER
NATHAN MILLER
ADAM MILLNS
JOHANNES MIRBACH
THOMAS MITCHELL
CATH MOLDAUER
DAVID M. MOLDAUER
PETER MOLYNEUX
ANDREW MONTGOMERY
DANIEL MOORE
IAN D. MOORE
NIGEL MOOREHEAD
PAUL, HENRY & PAT MORGAN
ELLIOTT MORLEY
MIKE MORLEY
ALAN MORRIS
DAVID S. MORRIS
SCOTT MORRISON
ZOE MORT
SOPHIE MORTIMER
THEO MORTON
PHIL MOSELEY
CHRISTINE MOSS
RONAN MULLAN
SEAN MULLANE
BRYONY MURPHY-GOTHARD
CHRISTOPHER MULLINS
DANIEL MURPHY
JONATHAN MURPHY
MARGARET MURPHY
ROBERT MURPHY
SEAN MURPHY
DON MURRAY
JOHN MURRAY
MYLES MURRAY
PAUL MURRAY
RABANNE MURRAY
TREVOR MURRAY

STEVEN MYCOCK
TERRY MYCOCK
TONY MYERS
MZINGA
SANJAY NAIR
B. NARENDRAN
VIC NAUGHTON
DEAN NEEDHAM
LEWIS JOHN NEEDHAM
MR STEWART NEEDHAM
FRANK NELSON
ARRON NICKLIN
NICOLE
BRIAN NIXON
PAUL NIXSON
STEVE NORTH
SUE NORTON
CHRIS NOWELL
MICHAEL O'BRIEN
JASON O'CONNOR
MARK O'CONNOR
MARK G. O'DONNELL
ROWAN O'DOUGHERTY
DAVID O'HALLORAN
JOHN O'HALLORAN
JOHN O'KEEFE
JOHN O'MAHONY
JULIE O'MAHONY
MANDIE O'MALLEY
PAUL O'ROURKE
AOIFE O'SULLIVAN
MATTHEW OAKES
CARL ODE
PETER ODE
MICK OGDEN
WILLIAM OKINE
CHIMA OKORONKWO
PAUL OLDHAM
SIMON ORMSTON
MICHAEL DAVID OWEN
STEWART RACHEL & RYAN
PAISLEY
NIGEL PALLANT
JOSHUA PARDOE
SIMON PARKER
STEVEN PARKER
MURRAY PARR
MICK PARRY
BERNARD PARSLEY
MATTHEW PARSLEY
NIGEL PATRICK (PADDY)
ELLA PATTERSON
PAULA & RIO

SONIA PEACOCK
SHAUN PEARCE
CONNER PEARS
KEVIN PEEK
MAUREEN PELHAM
MATTHEW PEMBERTON
NAT PENDLE
JAMES THOMAS PENDLEBURY
COLIN PERRY
KEVIN PERRY
PETER
MR G. PEXTON
MARK PHILLIPS
RHYS PICKEN
RONALD PIELOOR
SEAN PIERSE
MICHAEL PIKE
DANIEL STEPHEN PILKINGTON
GEORGE ELLIOTT PILKINGTON
MATTHEW CHARLES
PILKINGTON
KASAMA PLOCK
FRED POLLITT
CHRIS POOLEY
WILLIAM POTTER
CHRISTINE POWELL
STEPHEN POWER
NATHAN PREECE
CLIVE PRESCOTT
TREVOR PRICE
BRENDA PRITCHARD
CAIUS DAVID PRITCHARD
STEPHEN PRITCHARD
MAZ QAYYUM
DECLAN QUINN
ALAN RALPH
ALAN, JOHN & MICHAEL
RAMSBOTTOM
ANDREW RAMSBOTTOM
BEN RAMSDEN
RAY
ANDREW WILLIAM RAYNER
MICKEY REAY
ANDREW REDHEAD
IAN REDHEAD
GEORGE REED
DANIEL REGAN
KAREN REIL
JOHN RENSHAW
TERRY RENSHAW
TREVOR REVIS
HARVEY REYER
MATT REYNOLDS

JOHN RHODES
DYLAN RHODES'MURPHY
JAMES RHYS RYAN
BILL RICHARDS
ALAN RICHARDSON
GREGG RICHARDSON
TONY RICHARDSON
KEVIN RIDLEY
PHILLIP RIGBY
CARL RIGGALL
SAM RIGGANS
JOYCE RILEY
JO RITZEMA
PETER ROBERTSHAW
CHAS ROBINSON
WAYNE SHAW ROBINSON
CALLUM ROGERS
DAVID CONNOLLY ROGERS
JOHN ROGERS
TERRY ROGERSON
ROSS
DAVID ROSTRON
COREY ROWLINSON
JEZ ROWSON
DAVE RUDERHAM
ERIC RULE
DOUGLAS RUTTER
STEPHEN RUTTER
DANIEL PATRICK RYAN
EMMA RYAN
JON RYAN
TONY RYAN
IBRAHIM BABATUNDE SADIQ
GAVIN SAGAR
SALFORDMG1177
AQEEL SALLU
ADAM JAMES SANDERSON
PETER SANSOM
ANNE PATRICIA SAUNDERS
JACK SAWARD
MARK SCANLAN
JOHANNES SCHNAPP
DAVID K. SCHOFIELD
ELLIOTT SCHOFIELD
MELISSA J. SCHOFIELD
SAM SCHOFIELD
KYLE-THOMAS SCOTT
SEAN
DAVID C. SEARLE
VINNY SEBASTIAN
EMMA SENIOR
MARK SENIOR
GARY R. SEWELL

PETER SEYMOUR
ALAN & DANIEL SHALLICKER
MARGARET SHANNON
ASHOK SHARMA
JOE SHARPLES
ANDY SHARRAD
DON SHAW
DOUGIE SHAW
IAN SHAW
KELBY SHAW
MARTIN SHAW
WAYNE SHAW ROBINSON
KAREN SHEARD
CHRISTOPHER LEE SHENTON
JACQUELINE ANNE SHENTON
JONATHON TERRENCE
SHENTON
KYLE JACOB SHENTON-COX
GUY SHELDON
SAMMY SHEPPARD
PAUL SHERLOCK
AKIKO SHIOKAWA
ANDREW SHOREMAN
MARCUS SIDAWAY
STEVEN SILVESTER
FRANK SIMCOCK (AUS)
SIMON
OLLY SIMPSON
STEPHEN DAVID SIMPSON
SUE SIMPSON
BRIAN SIMS
MICHAEL SIMS
MIKE SIMS
IQBAL SINGH
DAVID SKELHORN
MRS SKELTON
PAUL SKORSKI
TONI SLOANE
VICKY SMEDLEY
ALEATHIA SMITH
BRIAN SMITH
DARLO KEV SMITH
DAVID SMITH
DIANNA MAY SMITH
KEITH M SMITH
PAUL ANTHONY SMITH
ROLAND SMITH
STEVE SMITH
ASHLEY JOHN SNOWBALL
THOMAS SPENCER
STEVE SPENCER
STEPHEN BUSTER SPRINTALL
CALLUM SQUIRES

RUSSELL STALEY
TOM STARKEY
DAVID STARRS
BRYAN IAN FREDERICK
STATHAM
GEMMA L. STEWART
MR W. J. STOCKMAN & MRS
EILEEN STOCKMAN
GARY STOKES
CHRISTINE GLORIA STONE
JASON SAMUEL STOTT
LUKE STORR
NATHAN STORR
STUART
JAMES SUDWORTH
STEVE SULLIVAN
PHILLIP SUMNER
JAMES SURRIDGE
JOHN SUTTON
PAT SUTTON
JAMES SWEENEY
MATHEW SWIFT
ANTHONY TAKER
MARK TALLIS
AARON TANNER
JOHN TATE
CARL TAYLOR
PAUL TAYLOR
TOM TEMPLE
MICHAEL TENNYSON
DAVE THOMAS
MARTIN THOMPSON
IAN THORNTON
JODIE THORNTON
TIGHWAD
JONATHAN TOMBS
ANDREW TOMKINSON
KEVIN TONGE
ROSEMARIE TONGS
KAREN TORRINGTON
ROBERT TOWNLEY
KAY TOWNSEND
KEITH TOWNSEND
IAN TRAVIS
MARY TREANOR
MATT TRENBIRTH
CHRIS TURNER
JOHN TURNER
JONA TURNER
KEN TUTTY
EDDIE TWEMLOW
BRENDAN TWOMEY
SEAN TWOMEY

SCOTT UNSWORTH
JAGVIR SINGH UPPAL
REG UPTON
STEFAN USANSKY
AARON VANDERMARK
ANDREW VARDEN
ROBERT JOSEPH VERITY
MICHAEL VINCENT
JAN DE WAL - A'DAM RED
ADI WALKER
ANDREW JOHN WALKER
ANDREW THOMAS WALKER
CHRIS WALKER
DANIEL WALKER
DAVID WALKER
DEBBIE WALKER
GEORGE WALKER
LEE WALKER
LIONEL WALKER
MARC WALKER
MARTIN JOHN WALKER
OLIVER WALKER
TERENCE WALKER
SAM WALL
ELLIOT WALLACE
JORDAN WALLACE
SAM WALLACE
GRAHAM WALLBANK
GARETH WALMSLEY
DEBRA WALSH
MORGAN WALSH
NEIL WALSH
MALCOLM WALTON
RAY WALTON
CHRIS WARD
JIM WARD
OLIVIA WARD
TERRY WARD
LEWIS WARDLE
JOSHUA WARE
GLYN WARRINGTON
BRIAN WARWICK
JAMES MICHAEL WATSON
NICK WATSON
DANIEL WATTS
CRAIG WEBB
BEN WEBSTER
ROBERT WELLS
ROY WELSH
MICHAEL GRAHAM WHARTON-
PALMER
MICK WHEATCROFT
DENIS WHITE

IAN CHRISTOPHER WHITE
NICHOLAS JEREMY WHITEHAND
ALAN HENRY WHITEHEAD
JAMES WHITTAKER
MARTIN WHITTAKER
MARK WHITTLE
TYLER WHITTON
ALAN WILKINSON
LEE WILKINSON
MICHAEL T. WILKINSON
PETE WILKINSON
ADAM WILLIAMS
BERNADETTE WILLIAMS
CAROLYN WILLIAMS
DAVID THOMAS WILLIAMS
JOAN WILLIAMS
ROBERT WILLS
NATHAN WILMOTT
DYLAN WILSON
PETER ANTHONY WILSON
OLI WINTON
ROBERT WINTON
THOMAS WITHERS
DAVID WOOD
ODETTE WOOD
PETER WOOD
RICHARD F. WOOD
DAVE WOODWARD
KARL WOODWARD
RICHARD WOODWARD
COREY WORSWICK
GORDON WRIDE
CAROL WRIGHT
DAVID WRIGHT
JARED WRIGHT
KEN WRIGHT
PHIL WRIGHT
DANIEL WYCHRIJ
CRAIG WYLIE
PAUL YARDLEY
HOWARD & JOSHUA YATES
KENNY YEARSLEY